The Ambassadors of the
Texas Hill Country

Photos and text by John F. Aceti

Jane,
Enjoy the read.
Best wishes,
John F. Aceti

Copyright © 2012 by John F. Aceti
First Edition –October 2012

ISBN
(Hardcover) 978-1-4602-0531-0
(Paperback) 978-1-4602-0529-7
(eBook)   978-1-4602-0530-3

Produced by:

FriesenPress
Suite 300 – 852 Fort Street
Victoria, BC, Canada V8W 1H8

www.friesenpress.com

Distributed to the trade by The
Ingram Book Company

TABLE OF CONTENTS

This book is dedicated to my wife Carol, who is my best friend, traveling partner, discussion partner, best critic, and best advisor. The book was written because of her encouragement and support.

Acknowledgments

I would like to thank all the individuals who willingly shared their personal life stories with me.

A personal thank you to all the transcribers: Eloise Wiles, Tina Gonzalez, Ann Buck, Carol Aceti, and Ashleigh Kelm;

To my editor, Skye Alexander, for her great assistance;

To my family members for their continued support;

To photographer K. M. Peterson for his photograph of me;

To my grandchildren Michael, Macy, and Addison as they begin their life stories;

To Mike Wilson of River's Edge Gallery for his technical assistance;

To Phil Houseall for identifying people to interview;

And to all Texans who help make Texas a great place to live.

Finally, I would like to thank my publishing team at Friesen Press. To Melissa Hall, Erin McCullough, Sean Ho, thank you for all of your encouragement and support.

Praise for

The Ambassadors of the Texas Hill Country

"By exploring the individual stories of Texans, this book captures the larger-than-life yet deeply personal spirit of this impressive state. From immigrants, public health workers, international artists to homemakers, chefs to small town entrepreneurs, the breathtaking diversity of narratives continually draws readers to ponder what matters most in their lives and locations. Take this book, settle in a cozy chair, and savor every story. You're in the Texas Hill Country now." — Shanxi Omoniyi, online editor and content manager, The Christian Foundation for Children and Aging (CFCA), Shawnee, Kansas "I was captivated by the individual stories of those interviewed—some heartwarming, some sad, but all intriguing. The local Chambers of Commerce would do well to use these stories of folks who have come to the Hill Country to promote all the area has to offer—warmth, beauty, and most of all, the many passions of those who live here." —Craig Sinesiou, instructor, St. Bonaventure University, Cuba, New York "*The Ambassadors of the Texas Hill Country* provides a fascinating account of why individuals from various areas of the United States and the world ended up settling in the Texas Hill Country. It makes one want to hop a plane and relocate to that part of Texas." —Daniel Mateleska, president/owner of MW Medical Management Associates, LLC, Cumberland, Rhode Island "Nature created the Texas Hill Country and gave it its physical features. The people who reside in the Hill Country give it its character. John Aceti sets out to tell the story of why people were attracted to the Hill Country. He tells their stories and gives the reader an insight into what makes the Hill Country a great place to live." —Doug Whinnery, Retired USAF Officer, Kerrville, Texas "*The Ambassadors of the Texas Hill Country* is a collection of stories that not only provide insight into why people come to Texas and love it, but also why they see the world as they do. From Germany to Chiapas, the ambassadors come. The words that John Aceti collected capture a moment in time, which makes the book invaluable as an historical document. Those same words entertain us, pull at our heartstrings, and even inform us! As someone who has collected the stories of many people in Texas music, I love this collection, which gives fresh eye wisdom to what we know and love about Texas. To quote Gary P. Nunn, "That's what I like about Texas." —Kathleen Hudson, Ph.D, Schreiner University, and Texas Heritage Music Foundation, Kerrville, Texas, www.texasheritagemusic.org

Foreword

Before my wife and I decided to make our retirement home in the Hill Country, we read a dozen or more of the hundreds of books that have been written about this unusual area of Texas. We had the freedom to go anywhere in the world, but the Hill Country kept popping up on everybody's list of the best places to retire. So we checked it out thoroughly.

All kinds of books have been written on the subject, from bona fide history to histrionic (and barely believable) legends. These books extol both real and imagined benefits of visiting and even putting down roots here—great climate, proximity to big-city markets, but without the traffic and pollution that come with them, scenery and sights unlike any within 600 miles, world-class museums, and school systems to rival the best. The list goes on and on.

We investigated all these things, and found that most of the literature and Chambers of Commerce/Visitors' Centers promotional material missed the point of the real allure of the area: the people. A veritable United Nations of countries and cultures blend here in what we could only think of as almost a metaphysical stew. Nobody talks much about it, concentrating instead on the Prussian immigrants and their land grants from Stephen F. Austin, and the once Republic of Texas. There's talk of Native Americans, mostly the Antelope Comanche led by Pita Nocona and his half-Anglo son, Quanah Parker, and their many skirmishes with the old Texas Rangers who—truth be told—were largely a bunch of hard-drinking idlers with nothing much to do. A sentence crops up here and there in the histories about Mormon settlements along the Pedernales and Guadalupe Rivers. And, of course, the ubiquitous Mexicans migrating north with the cattle drives.

Even today, the diversity of those who come to the Hill Country is hardly noticed and seldom spoken of or written about—until John and Carol Aceti arrived in Kerrville from Upstate New York. John and Carol are clearly "people persons." Five or six years ago while John and I were in Mexico working on a Rotary economic development project he first brought up the idea of creating a book about the people who have come to the Hill Country. He believed these individuals had stories to tell—stories of what brought them here, how joining in the human diversity of the area had affected them, and how the cultures they brought with them have affected the area.

Ambassadors of the

I thought it was a great idea, and I told him so.

Voilà! *The Ambassadors of the Texas Hill Country* was born. It chronicles the stories of more than fifty individuals, their accounts of the transitions from their roots to West Central Texas—in their own words. And that's what makes the stories extra special. The first-person accounts— some of them a sentence or two, others mini-biographies—of people from Asia, Africa, South America, Eastern and Western Europe, even Iceland, and all across the U.S. from California to Massachusetts. It's a potpourri, a microcosm of what America is all about, and it belies the rugged individualist reputation of Texas tall tales. For every story John, an expert photographer, has recorded the storyteller's image, and the pictures speak volumes.

Perhaps the stories might be told about almost any enchanting place in the U.S. Because, after all, in the final analysis it's the people who give a place its character, attraction, and reputation. But this book is about the real Hill Country of Texas: its people.

Their message to you, the reader, is "Y'all come."

—*George Arnold, author, Fredericksburg, Texas, 2012*

www.CIAcats.com

Introduction

The state of Texas, especially the Texas Hill Country, has seen a great influx of persons from other states as well as other countries. The U.S. Census Report from 2000–2010 points out that the population of Texas increased 20.6 percent as compared to 9.7 percent in the United States.

The median increase in population in the twenty-one counties of the Texas Hill Country was at 16.1 percent, though some have grown by much greater numbers. For example, Williamson County's population has skyrocketed by 69.1 percent, whereas Hays, Kendall, and Kerr Counties have experienced a 61 percent increase. Only three counties lost some population.

In this book I provide important insight into people from other states, as well as other countries, who have chosen to make the Texas Hill Country their home. I visited cities and towns in eleven counties of the Hill Country and interviewed people from fourteen different states and from nineteen countries.

My purpose was to discover why people selected Texas—and specifically cities in the Texas Hill Country—in which to live, work, or retire rather than someplace else in the country. I determined that obtaining an oral history of each person would allow readers to understand the many skills and talents these people have brought to the Texas Hill Country. These newcomers came with the American spirit of adventure, mobility, and entrepreneurship that will benefit everyone.

The question people most frequently asked me was, "How and where did you locate the people you interviewed?" I identified a number of them by my attendance at Rotary Club meetings, and by visiting Chambers of Commerce and Visitor Centers, post offices, police personnel, museums, businesses, barbershops, libraries, restaurants, and wherever people congregate.

I asked participants a series of questions, in order to document their personal lives from an early age to the present time. Interviews were held in private homes, restaurants, business offices, and one in a restored county jail. These interviews will allow readers to learn about real people, real ambassadors, and now real Texans.

The question I most frequently asked the individuals in this book was, "What attracted you to the state of Texas and especially to the Texas Hill Country?"

Ambassadors of the

The most memorable response came from a dear friend, Marion Schulnegger, a manager at the Inn of the Hills Resort and Conference Center in Kerrville, Texas. When I told her about my book and that question, she threw both arms high in the air and explained, "It's the big blue sky, the mountains, the desert, the ocean, the wildlife, the ranches, and most of all the people—they are the friendliest, amicable, hospitable, neighborly, and warmhearted people anywhere."

The people from other states and countries who settled here had no difficulty adopting these same attitudes into their lives. In fact, most of the people who moved here attribute their happiness living here to the Texans in their communities who welcomed them with open arms.

My journey through the Texas Hill Country to meet these wonderful ambassadors has proven time and again that treating each other with respect and kindness can certainly develop into solid relationships.

AUSTIN

Ambassadors of the

Peter Previte

Austin, Texas–Niagara Falls, New York

What attracted me to Texas was an invitation from my sister-in-law to visit at Thanksgiving time. We were very impressed with the total experience and held many discussions about moving here.

Our two children were living at home at that time. Anthony had just started high school and Kayla was in junior high. My wife and I discussed the impact the move would have on our kids and we knew staying in Niagara Falls had its limitations. I thought if we moved to Texas they'd have all kinds of opportunities and chances to do whatever they wanted. In Niagara Falls, you're very limited and nothing's going on. So, we said let's do it—and here we are nine years later.

I really enjoy the weather, the sunshine, the climate, and the people. There is such a mixed bag of people here. On the street where we live, my best friend is from Israel. The people next door are homegrown Texans from Midland. The city has a heartbeat, with wonderful activities, excitement, and action.

I had a good childhood, but it wasn't a bed of roses. My dad worked hard because he was self-employed and he was always a go-getter. My mom was a stay-at-home mom and housewife, which was typical of most women during the early sixties and seventies. During weekends and summer vacations I worked with my father in his snack food and vending distribution business, which included potato chips, pretzels, and peanuts. He had also inherited a business from his grandfather that he had worked at since he was a kid. It was called Cataract Washing Solutions, and I started working in it as soon as I was old enough to carry a glass jug.

I wasn't the most studious student, but I enjoyed school, and had a good time with my friends. In my teens I basically followed the same path, working with my father in his businesses, going to high school, enjoying my friends, and had a pretty typical family life. During high school I was on the track team and foot-ball team. I got in a little bit of trouble and mischief, some drinking and carrying on—typical teenage boy stuff. I enjoyed my teen years.

After high school, I decided not to go to college. The day after I finished high school another opportunity came along in the snack food business. A woman who had a Charles Chips vending business was looking to get out of it. I talked to my father about expanding the business, and I started with Charles Chips on my own and did that for ten years. The transition felt really weird. I found myself in the truck thinking, geez, I should be in school right now, I would be in my homeroom. I kept telling myself, I'm not in school anymore, I'm working. I'm self-employed.

I started off delivering potato chips and snack foods in what was known as the home delivery phase—delivering to people's homes. Later, of course, we branched out to stores, restaurants, and bars.

The business at that time was starting to decline, along with the city. Because of the population decline, bars and restaurants were closing down, which affected my business. I continued to run it on my own, after my dad passed away, for another year or so, but was finally forced to close the business.

I then worked with Mang's Fish Market for ten years. My good friend Butch brought me on there. He and I expanded the business and started selling fish fries, which was a huge success. But the economy at Niagara Falls declined again, so I left that business and moved to Texas.

My wife and I first came to Texas for a couple of "recon missions," as we called them, to see what we could do. We found a subdivision near where my sister-in-law lived and decided to build a home and maybe ranch here. We needed jobs, so we just sent out applications everywhere.

Ambassadors of the

I took the first job offer that came along, managing Cici's Pizza, but I only did that for two years. Now I am doing flood certifications. Anytime you buy property or a home or refinance you need a certificate stating that you are in or out of a flood zone, for flood insurance purposes. It's mandatory federally. If you are in a flood zone and you have a loan on your property, the banks require you to have flood insurance. That's what I do—I make the determination as to whether people are required to have insurance.

I cover a large geographic area—all of the United States and its territories. Am I kidding? No, I'm not, and I do it all from my desk here in Texas. Most transactions are done by computer and we have a staff of at least thirty in our company.

I have a very close family. My wife Donna and I have been married for twenty-four years. When we first came to Texas she started working with a mortgage company, which was the mortgage company and builders who built our house. She worked with them for a while, but she didn't feel comfortable with it because they were having her approve loans and get people to get loans, when she knew the people could not make their payments. Everyone already knows about the big bust our country is suffering and she was tired of it. She used to tell me about it long before it actually hit. She knew that everybody was signed up for a big fall. She said, "I just can't sit across the desk and look those people in the eye and say you're going to fail, you're not going to make it."

So she went to the First Texas Bank where she met Tracy, who became her best friend. Tracy's husband got me the job where I am now. Donna stayed there for a good many years until she got an opportunity to do something she's always loved to do—working with another custom homebuilder and doing the selections in interior design, paint colors, and helping with the design of it. That's what she does today, and she really loves it.

My older son Anthony recently graduated from Baylor University and went on to nursing school. He has his RN degree and he's working in a medical city neurotrauma unit in Plano, Texas. He really enjoys it and they are just thrilled with him. Many people ask about him and when we tell them what he's doing they can't believe a first-year graduate student was hired in that department. He has accelerated through that department, where he is on his own. They trust him completely and we're so proud of him.

My daughter Kayla is twenty years old and her big thing is animals. She is a vet tech and works at a veterinary clinic. We call her the animal whisperer because she's not just a dog or horse whisperer. Any animal she comes in contact with is a special event. One day she was driving down the road and there was a red-tail hawk lying on the road, and she went up to this hawk and whispered to it. She picked it up and brought it back to her truck and nursed it back to health. The hawk stayed around for a long time. It wouldn't let anybody come near Kayla and became very protective of her. She called him friend and every time he saw her he would get excited and fly down—people were just amazed that a red-tail hawk would be so taken to her. And she's that way with every animal—she's just amazing.

We would like her to pursue and stay in the vet tech business, but her big thing is horses. She wants to eventually get into equine training and breeding. She wants to become a cowgirl—she even rides bulls in the rodeo. You heard me right—bulls. In the rodeo. A twenty-year-old girl from Niagara Falls, New York. She scares us to death. Has she ever gotten hurt? Yeah, more times than she's shown us. She has been stepped on and gotten bruises. Does it bother me? Hell yes. I have to say she really has guts.

I told you a little bit about my father, whose name was also Peter. He was born and raised in Niagara Falls and worked hard all his life. And my mother Elaine, I forgot how they met, but it was in Niagara Falls—she still lives there. In fact, my mother still lives in the house where she grew up with her parents on Twenty-first Street. In her early years she worked for a bank.

What's my legacy to my children and the young people of today? Just live your lives and try to be good people, help people, work hard at your jobs and at what you do. Try to find something that you enjoy doing and do it to the best of your abilities. Love God and love your country and the great state of Texas. Other than that, just be loving and kind individuals. Try to make people happy and you'll find that you will make yourselves happy.

Mordechai Weisbrod

Austin, Texas-Neuburg, Germany

Before coming to Texas in 2002 I lived in California for a year and a half and prior to that in Florida. Texas was not something I thought about when I became an animator. As an animator for the last ten years I've animated films and worked with video game companies. When I lived in California from 2001 to 2002, my wife, Tiffany, and I thought California was super expensive for us, even though I worked for a very famous company, ILN, a George Lukas Company. There were five people in one apartment with one bathroom and the rent was $2,345 a month.

I was very fortunate to work on films such as *Star Wars* and *Men in Black*. During the second one I remember I felt trapped. It was work and come home, work and come home. I could not afford anything besides food and necessities.

I had a mentor there whose name was Martin, a very talented animator from Quebec. He used to work in Austin before going to California and he planned to move back to Texas. I was happy where I was. I learned tons and I graduated from Ringling College as an animator. The dream job for most students was to work for a film company, so I'd landed a perfect job. But after a year and a half,

I felt dead and thought maybe Martin was right. After thinking about it and talking it over with my wife, I decided we should at least look at it. I would talk to the same company that Martin interviewed with and see what it was like.

I came here for an interview and spent the weekend with a friend. I called Tiffany after the interview and said, "We are moving here." I really liked it and the people were friendly. The pace was slower. I felt I needed something more relaxing than just work.

I was born in 1973 in Germany and I lived there for seven years with my mom and my dad and my two brothers. I spoke German fluently because I grew up speaking it. My parents spoke Hebrew all the time. I remember we were a very loving family. My mom was a stay-at-home mom. She was there when I came home from kindergarten. My dad was a pediatrician. My dad is a very smart man, very smart, reads nonstop. My mom was very street smart. She is the one I come to, to this day, if I need advice about my marriage, my kids, what to do about my finances—any of my life decisions. My dad is more into intellectual conversation. I am very close to my brothers, who are younger than me. One lives in New York and is an opera singer and a performer; the other one lives in Israel.

The big thing for us was when we moved from Germany to Israel. My grandparents were all Holocaust survivors. My grandmother said she could not live in Germany after going through the Holocaust.

It was great getting used to the life in Israel. I did not speak the language. I came to Israel in July or August and my parents tell me that within a month or so I asked them to stop speaking to me in German and to only talk to me in Hebrew, which I regret because I have lost my German. But after three months it was easier for me, once I picked up the language.

I was a good student. I studied well. I was a student who was influenced by the environment. I'm competitive. If the environment provides me with competition, I'm there trying to be the best. But if the environment is a little easier, not a competitive environment, I tend to slide too. When I was bored with school I got into art a bit. There was something about art that let me escape when things got boring.

"Mookie" is the nickname I was born with. Especially in Israel, it is a common dog's name. It's like Fido here, it's that bad. When I was a kid, it traumatized me when I went to a new class and the teacher read the names for the first time. When a teacher stated "Weisbrod, Mookie" everybody laughed.

Oddly enough, my teen years are almost erased from my brain. I don't know why. If you asked me the name of one of my middle school teachers, I couldn't tell you. I talked to my wife about this. She is very good about dates, where she was, what she ate, that sort of thing. It seems like a forgotten era. I think at that time my parents weren't involved with what I was doing—I could do whatever I wanted. They probably did not care because I was a good boy so they trusted me a lot. I still keep in touch with some of my friends, but as far as the teachers I could not name one.

When I was a kid in Israel, sports were not as big. I used to play soccer but I wasn't very good at it. I used to hang out with the guys because I'm competitive and I tend to take things a little more seriously.

After high school, in Israel, everyone has to go into the army. For men, it was for three years so from the age of eighteen to twenty-one I was in the army. I was in the anti-aircraft unit. At one point I became a drill sergeant. I had a good time in the army, a really good time, I enjoyed it.

In the army I met a guy who was an animator and he taught me how to animate. I was so excited when I came home on vacation and talked to my mom and told her my friend was going to teach me.

Right away she asked, "How much are you going to pay him?"

I said, "He's my friend, why should I pay him?"

"If you don't pay him he won't teach you. He may do it once or twice, but soon enough other things will come into play and you will become less and less important. Not because he is not a good friend, but because he has other priorities in life. Pay him. A friend for life, pay him."

So I paid him. I paid him well.

In 1995, I was done with the army. In 1996, I talked to my parents and said I really wanted to become an animator. I wanted to do it for a living and I thought I could. I thought I had to prove to the world that I was worthy so I needed to get a degree. I told my mom I needed to get a degree in business and that way I could also study art. She told me, "No, no, study art if that is what you really want to do, study art."

I looked for about a year. I searched every school in Israel for one that would teach me what I thought I needed. I thought every school would only teach me about software. I thought I would need something more because software is only a book. I can read a book myself. After about a year of searching, working at odd jobs like at Home Depot, I told my mom I didn't think there was a school in Israel that offered what I needed.

I went to Tel Aviv and talked to the American Embassy, and I talked to the German Embassy, and the British Embassy. I told them I wanted to be an animator and asked if they could help me. The American Embassy was amazing. They told me to come back in a week, and in a week they gave me a list of all the schools in the United States that teach animation and they showed me which companies, also. It was amazing—all these colleges and companies. Out of all these colleges, I chose two and I ended up going to the Ringling School of Art and Design in Sarasota, Florida.

That was a very good school. I'd read about it before and I knew it was great, but my friend told me there was no way I could make it. I applied and I was accepted. That was 1995–1996. I was really thrilled. But I had to wait a whole year to start because I missed my deadline. I wasn't too aware of deadlines, rules, and stuff like that. Once again, I kept working at odd jobs, selling lamps—another one of those time passing periods—then I moved to Sarasota, Florida with two suitcases.

I graduated four years later.

My wife is Tiffany Danielle Smith and I met her at college, at Ringling. We both started the same school year. She was in illustration and I was in animation, but we were in different classes. I remember noticing her during our freshman year. She was a little bit of troublemaker. Her teacher kicked her out of drawing class and put her in another drawing class because she and her friends were too loud and rowdy. So they brought her to our class and I was pretty happy about that.

We dated for a long time, since 1997. I'm a little old-fashioned when it comes to decision-making, so we got married in 2004. We have two children. Hanna is three years old and Oliver is almost eleven months.

What kind of legacy do I want to leave for my children? I think it's really important to make sure they know that always, somebody is there for whatever reason, for whatever they need, no matter what they do. I'm hoping to be somebody they remember as a caring person.

BANDERA

Horst Pallaske

Bandera. Texas-Naehrschuetz. Germany

I was born in Naehrschuetz, Germany, which is near the city of Wohlau. It originally was Germany, then East Germany, and then Poland. Now I live in Bandera, Texas, the cowboy capital of the world, although I am not a cowboy.

It wasn't an attraction, it was the U.S. military that brought me to Texas first and that's how I got to know Texas. I was stationed in the Army at Fort Sam in San Antonio, and I was in the Army for twenty-three years. We had a bulletin board that listed all the duties you had and on the other side it told you the places to visit that were interesting as well as the places that were off-limits. At that time the whole town of Bandera was off-limits. So naturally, as a young man, I hopped on the next bus to come here and see why it was off-limits.

I found a wonderful town here and I've enjoyed it since day one. Naturally, I couldn't stay here then except just a weekend or two. I got shipped to Southeast Asia. But I loved the town.

Ambassadors of the

With help from some friends I got back here. We were stationed together in Fort Sam and I stayed in contact with them for over twenty years. I came to visit just before I retired and said I wanted to live somewhere around here. San Antonio wasn't a choice for me anymore—Bandera was where I wanted to be. I've been here twenty years. I love it.

When I was a kid I was in the hospital. I had tuberculosis and all kinds of children's illnesses. I was exactly one year and one day in the hospital, it was right after the war in 1945. The doctors told my mom I would never make it, but the day before I left I was eating like a pig.

We lived in a refugee camp in Germany. It used to be a Polish prison camp for Polish soldiers and after the war that's where we lived. There was no life of luxury or anything like this. As a child, you don't know much better, so we made the best of it. Of all things, we played cowboys and Indians. The only thing that really bothered me at that time was we were hungry, we didn't have much food. American soldiers looked out for us, they came into our camps and brought us food. You know it's just like today—the American soldiers have not changed, children are always number one for them they took care of us. If it wasn't for them I would've lost my life.

I was a wild young man, ran around in the woods, had a bicycle, and rode all over Europe on that bicycle. I belonged to an amateur acting group, which I really enjoyed. It was something I had never experienced and from day one I loved it.

In Germany, the way you selected a job was the German government came to your school when you were about thirteen and gave you an aptitude test. According to the aptitude test, they said I would qualify to become a machinist. So my family sent me to machinist school and I also worked as an apprentice at the same time. I had three and a half more years to go for a machinist. When I finished, I worked as a machinist for a short while.

In Germany at that time the equivalent to high school was fifth grade. When I came to this country and people asked me how many years I went to school I said eight years in Germany, and they said it was equivalent to high school.

I came to the U.S. in November 1963, the day after John F. Kennedy got assassinated so it was a very scary situation. I was nineteen. I was in a boat with mostly immigrants on it, and we all thought they would turn the boat around and send us back home. But nope, we came into New York to the harbor and the customs people were very respectful.

I came here because of the Americans I met in the refugee camp. I got to know an American G.I. there and I thought if an American soldier can be like this the rest of the country must be much better. I came by myself. My mom stayed there. She didn't want to come with me. She was afraid of flying, she was afraid of going on the boat. I can understand this, but I had to leave.

My dad was missing in the second war. I can't say much about him, I was too small to know him. I was born in 1944 and he went missing in '45. He was originally what you call a river boatman. He was in the German Navy first, then somehow he ended up in the German Army and got wounded in France. They sent him to the hospital, and Russians started coming in. That's the last we heard. I had a sister, but she passed away before I was born. I know nothing about my grandparents, never have seen them once.

I have a bunch of cousins that live mainly on the west side, and I keep in contact with them. The ones mainly on the east side I stopped having contact with because of the way they took advantage of my mom. When war was on everybody needed things, and they wrote her asking could she send this or that. My mom didn't have much money but she tried to help them as much as she could. As soon as the war was done, she never heard from them, no Christmas card, no birthday card, nothing. So why should I stay in contact with these people?

Out of my twenty-three years in the Army I was seventeen years stationed in Germany. Because of my language ability, I was a very inexpensive interpreter. I was also stationed in Bitburg, Germany in 1990 and I was there for nine years.

When I first came to the U.S., I got a job through an accident. I was in a restaurant and the waiter couldn't understand what I wanted. A gentleman there caught on that I was from Germany so he motioned me to keep my seat and he would be right back. He came back with two little dictionaries, German–English, English–German. We had a conversation that way and he found out I was a machinist. That lit up his eyes and he said he had a newspaper in Minnesota and he needed a machinist. So that's where I worked for several years, until I got drafted.

Minnesota was too cold, but as a young man it didn't bother me that much. It was a good job, very interesting. And the Minnesota people are actually like Texas people, very friendly, very warm, just politically they're opposites.

I was drafted into the U.S. Army. I had to go to Virginia and take my job training there, and I had to take basic training. They didn't know what to do with me. Everybody got shipped to Southeast Asia except two of us. The other one was a conscientious objector. We waited for weeks, then I got a call to go to Fort Sam and I stayed there until I got shipped to Southeast Asia. I was in Vietnam, going back and forth. I could've stayed in the Army longer, but after twenty-three years I had enough of it. I was in Germany when I left the service. My mom was still alive and I promised her I would stay in Germany as long as she lived, but it wasn't long after that she passed away.

I made arrangements with the friends I had here. I came to visit first and looked around a bit. I had so much fun here in Bandera that I told them to find a house for me. They did, and that's where I live right now.

I've been the mayor here for three years. I have twenty-something people working for me, and I'm responsible for them keeping their jobs. There are 953 people in the city of Bandera, and when they need help I'm there for them. Trying to fix the sewer and water, trying to get it up to date, get the streets fixed, while also trying to keep property taxes down—that is very important. That is why I got into politics. I've been trying to fight property taxes from day one. Actually, in the third year I was here, all of a sudden they started raising property taxes tremendously. And I couldn't do anything, so I said "If you can't beat them,

Ambassadors of the

join them." I became a councilman first. So far I've been keeping my word. This is my second term as mayor, it's a two-year position. I got re-elected with 80 percent of the vote.

I belong to the Lions' Club and to the Optimist Club. Whatever needs help here I usually help out. I'm also the president of the Economic Development Corporation. I take care of the city park—it's one of my pet projects and the city park always looks good. From the day I became a council member I started working on it. I'm proud of that, that I got a real good group. I'm also a board member of the Frontier Museum. We're the only museum in Texas that has a shrunken head.

Streetlights got done because when I came here, across where the old porch was, a man got hit by a car and he passed away—the driver said he couldn't see him. That particular spot was very dark, so we talked to the Economic Development Corporation and we said, "We need to put streetlights here." Anything I do is always for this town. When I see something getting done it makes me feel good.

I fit in very well here, why exactly I can't say. Maybe because the people that immigrated here came from the area where I was born. They said no foreigner has ever fit in so well. From day one I considered this my home. The whole town is my family. I don't really go on vacations—I say I *am* on vacation.

I like the honky tonks here, I enjoy country and western music, and I know just about every cowboy that is a musician in this town. I've had many good times with them. Archy Blues is a historical place all by itself—it looks like a museum. It's a place you walk in as a total stranger and walk out as a friend. We have a wine and cheese place here, and they have German beers on draft—I enjoy that.

I'll be mayor for one more year. Then maybe just kick back for a while and look around. I just got over cancer. I'm still not myself but I'm getting a lot better. I'll stay in Bandera, though—I won't be leaving. I will find something to do, I don't have a plan. I will keep working on the house to improve it. Otherwise, I'm sure somebody is just waiting for me. I had a phone call one time, and they said, "Congratulations." I said, "For what?" They said, "You are now working for the boys' and girls' club. You know, that's just the way it works around here.

There's supposed to be another city in Texas that calls itself the cowboy capital of the world. I think we have more cowboy events going on than anyone else. Celebrate Bandera, that's a huge thing. When the longhorns are taken down the main street, the event planners and ourselves make sure that nothing is going to happen, nobody gets hurt. Also we have our Riverfest, which is sometimes outrageous. One time there was a float with three horses and riders on it. They were doing very well until just at the end when some horse made a move and all the horses fell in the water with the riders on top of them. The people watching thought it was staged. But we knew it was an accident. Then there's Hunters' Weekend, and all kinds of little festivals.

Let me say something, I do have some dealings with some locals, and here in Bandera we don't need a contract, we just need a handshake and look each other in the eye. This is what I like to see. Walk over, learn as much as you can, be honest with yourself and everybody else. One thing I like to live by is: do upon others what you want others to do upon you. If people want to live life that way they will find out life is beautiful.

Georgia Schoelles, Store Clerk

Bandera, Texas–Athens, Greece

God, family, and friends—an amazing combination that will make you a stronger and better human being.

Monica Hanger

Bandera, Texas–Tuxtla, Gutierrez, Chiapas, Mexico

I am the daughter of a single mother, but I was practically raised by my grand-mother in central Mexico. She was very attached to traditions and old customs, so she shared with me all this cultural heritage and probably didn't know that it was cultural heritage. But she shared those customs and traditions and her passion for Mexico with me. I have fond memories of going with her to the market and different places around the neighborhood. I used to go with her to buy food and toys. My grandmother was a great influence in my life. She influenced one of the biggest loves and passions in my life: the ancient cultures of Mexico. I was particularly attracted to the Mayan civilization because my mother told me that my father was born in Andalusia, Spain.

My grandmother always picked me up at school. When I was a little girl, I went to a bicultural school. My mother always considered it very important for me to learn a foreign language. I started studying French and then English

Ambassadors of the

when I was a little girl. It was kind of difficult, but I guess I never knew that and nowadays I don't regret it at all. I have very few memories about my childhood, though. Part of it was spent in a place near Mexico City.

When I was a teenager, instead of having a quinceanera party I wanted to have a trip to the Mayan area in my country. My mother couldn't give it to me because she refused to travel with me—she was always busy working. I was a minor, therefore, I couldn't travel on my own and it was a very frustrating time for me. Finally, at the age of eighteen I was able to travel to the southernmost part of my country, Chiapas. I fell in love with it and realized, this is where I belong.

I finished high school and then went into college. I saved all the money because I received an allowance from both of my parents. My father was not with me, but he sent money and he paid my college tuition. I traveled every summer to the Chiapas area just to be close to the Mayan Indians and to the Mayan ruins. I really enjoyed that so much and I have the best memories of that time. I met many friends and established long-lasting connections with them. It was the highlight of my college years, going into the southern area and being with the Mayans. I loved that.

I wanted to study anthropology because I always liked the Meso-American cultures. But my mother didn't support that. We lived near Mexico City and there was no school there. Colleges in Mexico don't usually have dormitories or big campuses like here, so it was very difficult for me to commute. I didn't have a car and I was very young. My mother didn't want me living in the communities of the south and in the mountains of southern Mexico. I'd always liked languages, particularly the Spanish language, and I have some talent for words. I don't have any talent for numbers, I'm not very good at mathematics. So I decided to study linguistics and translation.

When I finished college and passed the test, I had to work. I wanted to study for a master's degree, but I didn't have the money and I needed to work. I was not feeling very happy in my house. My mother was supportive, but she was not really affectionate because she was on her own. She was overwhelmed with the stress of supporting my sister and me because she was a single mother in Mexico. She didn't have a degree so she had to work long hours to support us.

I started teaching Spanish to native speakers. Some people helped me to start working for the Department of Education, and I taught Spanish, how to write correctly, and to write reports. My first students were mainly secretaries or people working in offices who needed to write reports or letters. I taught them spelling and composition. That was my first job.

Following that I wanted to work at a university, college, or high school. I applied for a job at the Technological Institute of Chiapas, which is the name of the state where I was living, and the people who were in charge of hiring teachers told me I had to pass a test. This test is what we call in Spanish an Opposition Test and you had to give a class in front of a jury or judges. Based on that and answering some questions, they may give you the job. I was very young, about twenty-two, but I said to myself, "I'm going for it." I did and I passed the test.

Then they called me and told me I had the job. I accepted and I taught there. I had mixed feelings about the job because this technological institute is more directed toward technical stuff, and more like science. I am not very good at mathematics and physics and science, so that is not exactly my field. I love art and history and sociology, and all social sciences and arts.

I wanted to continue working because I wanted to buy a newer and bigger car, and I was saving money there in Chiapas. I applied for a job in one of the most prestigious institutions in Mexico called the Technological Institute of Monterrey. It's a private institution, and it's one of the most expensive schools in Mexico. I got a job in the college of translation and I also taught translation and linguistics. I worked there for three years.

I then received a scholarship to attend a university in England to study English and to make evaluations for teaching English as a second language, with all expenses paid.

I also taught at the Teachers' School in Chiapas, where I trained teachers in linguistics. I had a wonderful job and I cannot complain about my career. An acquaintance I had in Tuxtla invited me to study and work in the city of Leo, in Central Mexico, in the state of Guanajuato, so I went there and I started studying English. I got my certificate as a teacher; although I had a degree I was not formally a teacher. I went to college there again, and I became an English as a Second Language teacher. I started working for a state university, for the stability, the tenure, and the benefits. Private schools in Mexico pay probably a little bit better, but they don't give you as many benefits. I worked at the state university in the neighboring state of Guanajuato in Central Mexico. I lived there and worked at the state university for six years.

That summer I decided to take some vacation time and I went to San Miguel by bus. On the bus I met a couple from Comfort, Texas. They weren't sure where to go once we arrived in San Miguel, so I volunteered to be their guide for the week. We became friends and we started exchanging e-mails. They invited me to visit them in Comfort, so I was able to get a visa and I went to Texas in July 2000.

My first impression of Texas was, "Oh God! This is so humid and hot and I cannot even run while I am here." One of my hobbies is running.

Although I went back to work in Mexico, the couple from Comfort suggested I come back to visit from January to March when it is cooler. I was having difficulties with my boyfriend, so I asked my school for a semester leave and I went back to Comfort.

I was not planning to stay, but decided this would be an excellent opportunity to improve my English. Because I liked to run and swim and there is no sports center in Comfort, the couple I knew offered to take me to The Family Sports Center in Kerrville. I went there one day and while I was swimming a gentleman started talking to me. Later on, he asked the couple for my telephone number and he asked me for a date. We started dating. I guess we fell in love and I decided to go through the immigration process. He was there, paying the immigration lawyer, following every single step.

Ambassadors of the

I got my Green Card, then I got my citizenship in 2006. We got married in 2007 because we wanted to have a nice wedding. We've been married for almost two years, but we have lived together for seven years.

My mother still lives in Mexico. She as well as my friends were surprised to hear I was now married and living in Texas. They know I love Mexico. But they also understand that I've found my husband here.

I teach at Club Ed, which is part of the Kerrville school system, and I always speak highly about my students. My husband is a geologist, but he specializes and he's a geophysicist. He's a consultant for oil companies. He has his office in Bandera. When I met my husband he already had a ranch in Bandera. I prefer to live in a small city like Kerrville. I don't like to live in the countryside. I like to go out, meet people, talk to people, teach, go to swimming or aerobics classes. But that's where I met him and that's where he's got his office. He travels to San Antonio or to Dallas on a regular basis to meet with his bosses or clients.

I like to go to the marathons and half-marathons in San Antonio and Dallas. I enjoy running the marathons. Now I'm injured but I'm trying to continue. A marathon is 26.2 miles and a half-marathon is thirteen miles. I have run sixteen marathons and twenty-four half-marathons. I really enjoy it. I'm not really fast, but I've got endurance. I enjoy running here. When I run, when I train for these long races, I go to the back roads. In the back roads some neighbors know me, and they wave hello and ask me about my races and my miles.

My legacy to the young people of today? For the many students I taught in Mexico, I want them to love their country, and to do something for their country, not to see only the negative but to try to construct and build a better Mexico. I want always for them to be proud of their cultural heritage, not to deny it. How many countries in the world have Mexico's diversity in culture, customs, traditions, and folklore? I want this cultural heritage to prevail.

I would like the young people to have faith in their country. It's okay. It's easy just to leave, but I would like them not to leave and come here to work, but to stay in Mexico and work for Mexico —for a better Mexico. To study and to try to be better, to improve our education, to have a better ideology and work together. We really are honest and we really should work together and believe in each other so we can have a better country. It's not all corruption. I think we need to stand by ourselves in order to end this evil of Mexico. I would like them to be more aware of the importance of keeping the planet safe, not to destroy it. Being green—the trees, the wildlife, they're our lives! Erosion and lack of food, disease, and overpopulation—they need to be aware of that and take care of the planet. By destroying it we are destroying ourselves. We will collapse like the ancient Mayans.

Wild Bill Deene, Historian/ Storyteller

Bandera, Texas–Newark, New Jersey

Be ready to give of yourself, your time, and everything to anybody who needs help.

Ambassadors of the

BURNET

Kristin Bowman

Marble Falls, Texas–Syracuse, New York

I was born in Syracuse, New York and raised in Union Springs, New York, near Cayuga Lake in the Finger Lakes Region. My family moved to Union Springs when I was a year old. I lived there until I was about twenty-five or twenty-six years of age. It was a great place to grow up, a small town that still doesn't have a traffic light. I'm used to small towns and I like them.

When we moved to Union Springs, my parents bought a house that was large enough for my grandparents to live there also. It was a big house in the middle of town. I've lived my entire life with my maternal grandparents. My dad owned his own business and Mom and Dad worked together. He makes boat covers, does marine interiors, and upholstery work. They had a shop in the back of the house so they could pretty much work from home.

Ambassadors of the

I had one older sister. Our family is very small and both of my parents were only children, so I have no aunts or cousins—just the grandparents, my sister, and my parents. We grew up at a time where there were a lot of kids in the neighborhood and we ran around in the summers from morning to evening in a safe, small town. With my parents working right out of the house, they kept an eye on us, but growing up with my grandparents gave us a second pair of watchful eyes.

I went to a small public school there. I liked school. I wasn't the greatest student, but I enjoyed going. I had a lot of friends and I played sports from seventh to twelfth grade. I played soccer and basketball, and I guess being part of a team was great for me. I loved that.

In summers, we played summer soccer with coed teams and we always played at the park near the lake. It was a great place to be a kid.

As a teenager, we were still in the same school and played sports. I didn't have to get a job until I was in the eleventh or twelfth grade. I worked in the summers helping my dad. After that I worked at a local ice cream/mini golf place. I gained a little weight that summer eating ice cream but I really enjoyed it.

I was very lucky growing up. During the time my mom worked with my dad, she found a job working at one of the local places called Mackenzie Child Pottery. It was a very famous pottery place not too far from where we lived. She was the Director of Human Resources and she made pretty good money even when my dad's business was slow, so we were always comfortable. Having everyone under one roof was convenient—there was always someone around.

After high school I moved to Binghamton, New York and went to Broome Community College. My sister had gone there and so did my parents. Both of my parents are from the triple cities. My dad was born in Johnson City and my mom in Vestal—that's where they met. I got my associate's degree there in Business Administration. I started off as a marketing major and played soccer there for the team.

After I graduated from Broome I didn't really know what to do. I stayed in Binghamton because I had friends there and I had a job working at a local Super Eight Motel. This was perfect while I was in school because I worked the front desk and when there was no one to check in, I could do my homework. After a year, I applied to Binghamton University because I was originally going to be a sociology major. I was only there for one semester, then I decided to move back home to Union Springs. But when I left Binghamton I already knew I was going to get my master's in library science.

I then transferred to Wells College in Aurora, New York. It was an all-girls college at the time. It switched to coed while I was going there, which was interesting. I played for the soccer team as well. I got my bachelor's degree from Wells in religious studies with a concentration in human values. I needed a four-year degree before I could get my master's, so I just picked something that was interesting to me. I learned all about different religions, psychology, and anthropology. Everyone thought I was crazy—what kind of job can you get with a degree in religious studies? But I already had a plan.

I lived at home again, which was interesting being twenty-something and one of the older kids at the college. Most of the students went straight in at eighteen and graduated when they were twenty-one. I had taken some time off when I was at Broome, and I ended up going part-time for about a year, so it took me three years to get a two-year degree. And about another three years to finish up a four-year degree. I was about twenty-five or twenty-six when I got my bachelor's degree.

My mom and dad still own their own business, Deena's Cuts from Canvas in New York. They've been doing it for about thirty years, but they sold the shop where they used to work because the overhead was too much. Now Dad has a trailer he can take on location and still work.

My dad and my mom were always very involved with community. My dad was part of the Lions Club and served on the committee for the fun days, and they had car shows. He was also part of the zoning board. My mom was in quilt clubs. She helped put together the first preschool, in the church across the street from where I lived. She was also on the board for the local public library. She was actually the one who first suggested that I go to school for library science. And I thought, *what?* Librarian, I can't do that, that's too easy. She told me I used to love playing librarian with my sister when I was little. I thought, *that's true.* It ended up being a good fit.

They knew everybody because my dad had a shop right there in town. People would stop by and chat, and my mom would get annoyed because people were just coming in to talk to my dad and he had work to do. But he loves to talk to people and find out what's going on in town and the area. My parents are good people, definitely people I look up to and want to emulate. They've been married for thirty-some years. They have been very inspirational to me.

My grandma still lives with us in Marble Falls. My grandpa died a few years ago. They were definitely like a second set of parents. They knew me better than most people's grandparents. I think the most inspiring thing about my maternal grandparents was their relationship with each other. They were so in love and it killed my grandma when my grandpa died. She had been with him for so long. They met when they were fairly young and had such a great example of true love. That is what I'm looking for. I want someone like my grandpa. I want a relationship like my grandparents had because that's what life is all about.

I came to Marble Falls in a roundabout way. I never really enjoyed the winters. I found it difficult to drive in the snow. I used to like the snow days when I was younger. When I got out of high school, I went to college, but I was uncertain about my major. Finally I decided I wanted to be a librarian. I was accepted to the University of Arizona and I moved there to attend school. I got a part-time job at a public library while I was there. I lived there for about three years. Later, my parents decided to finally move out of New York state because of the cold weather and high taxes. They drove me to Tucson, but on their way home they took a detour through Texas and the Hill Country. My mom fell in love with it right way so that kind of planted the seed in her head of where they might want to move.

I moved to Marble Falls a little less than two years ago. I like it a lot and I love the weather. I didn't grow up here, but it seems being a Texan you'd be part of a club, and they're so welcoming and friendly that I automatically feel like I'm one of them now.

I had heard that the Herman Brown Free Library in Burnet was looking for an Assistant Director, so I submitted my application and a few days later I had an interview. Following that, I was notified that I received the appointment. I like my job. I love what I do. Working in the public library is great because I meet people I'd never meet some other way. I get to know people and what they do and what's going on in their lives.

I think the best thing about a job like this is I get to do everything. I'm not just helping people all day, I'm doing stuff in the back, I'm doing stuff up front with people, maintaining the collection, finding what we need. If people can't find something we order it for them.

I think the most important thing to know is that life is not what you plan it to be. You try to plan something, but that's not exactly what's going to happen. At the end, usually, what you didn't plan ends up being the best. Just go with it. Let life lead you where it's going to. Like fate, it knows more than you do.

A lot of the kids are stressed about what they're going to do, where are they going to go to school, how are they going to get in, how are they going to pay for it. They have to be working towards something, but it's not the end of the world if they don't get into their first-choice school. Or if they don't end up where they thought they would be. Because they're going to end up someplace pretty great. And they're going to be happy with it. I think it's best to know that life is going to unfold no matter how hard you work at it. It's best just to kind of go along for the ride and see where it brings you. I believe in the saying, it's not about the destination, it's about the journey—it's definitely been that way for me.

Mike Van Brocklin

Burnet, Texas-Orange County, California

I was born in Orange County, California—southern California—and raised in northern California in the Bay Area. I moved to Texas when I met my wife on a cruise ship in the Bahamas. I had never been to Texas and I had no intention of going there. I was a butcher and I had my time vested for retirement and I took a little time off to go see my mom and dad in Florida. A friend of mine called and said he was flying out that night and we were going on a cruise. When I got on the cruise I met my wife, Theresa. We got along and had a great time, and she lived in Burnet, Texas.

Ambassadors of the

While I was a kid living in California, my mom and dad wanted my brother and me to be raised in a smaller school environment. They felt that in a big city in California there were many problems with drugs in the schools and all the bad things that went on in the big city. They decided to move to the small town of Mexico, Missouri. We were raised there from when I was in fifth grade to eleventh grade. My dad's friend also moved there, and my dad worked at a nuclear plant in Calloway County.

It was a small town and it was really nice. I went fishing every day, because we lived in the country. I didn't really get to play sports because we lived so far out in the country. But, man, I loved my fishing every day. They call them "tanks" here in Texas, but in Missouri they are ponds and lakes. I probably had twelve of them around the area and fishing is what I did every day. Being raised like that and then seeing this town of Burnet, it kind of brought back all those memories.

Living in a small town was wonderful. I remember back in those days I got a $5-a-week allowance. I could buy five gallons of gas and one bottle of oil for my motorcycle for $5. I just basically rode my motorcycle to the ponds and lakes and fished and had a good time, and I wanted my kids raised like that.

I think school is the same anywhere you go, small towns, big towns. You always worry about what kids think about you. Mine was a good school, really good school.

My best friend lived in town and I helped him with his paper route. Remember when you'd tie the bag under the front of your bicycle and you'd fold the papers and sling them at the house? To him it was work, to me it was fun.

I did have responsibilities at home. My brother and I had to vacuum the house, do the dishes, take care of all the housework, it seemed like. Except for the laundry; we didn't do laundry. My mom cooked dinner, but my mom wasn't a very good cook and my brother and I, along with Dad, always said something about her cooking. I remember when I was thirteen we were teasing her about dinner and my mother said, "Y'all enjoy it because this is the last dinner I am cooking for you." We had to start cooking for ourselves.

I guess I was in about tenth grade or eleventh grade when my parents were thinking about moving to Honduras, on a little island called Roatan. My parents are Jehovah's Witnesses and they like to go preach a little bit. They like to go out and do ministry work. My mom also liked the adventure of being on a remote island, which was real primitive with a dirt runway. I had to pack water up to the house, and the electricity was unreliable and went off and on. I just hated the whole idea of leaving school. I mean, your junior and senior years are supposed to be your best years in high school. I had to take correspondence school in Roatan.

All I did on the island every day was snorkel and shoot lobster. I got so sick of eating lobster. I just wanted a McDonald's hamburger or candy bar, just anything. But I had to eat shrimp and fish and lobster every day. It made me so mad, and I complained and complained. We lived in this house up on stilts. I remember bats flew in the house at night—it was really primitive. We lived there once for a year and another time for six or eight months. I wanted to get out.

I left before my mom and dad. I was seventeen. I had a girlfriend in California at that time and her dad was the head butcher at a butcher shop at a big chain. My grandfather had just passed away. He was the president of the butcher's union of all of northern California, so that was a pretty good deal. I had connections, so I could get in. I started roofing while I waited for the butcher job to open up. Even though California heat is dry, it got to 105 up on the roof—it was cooking. When the butcher job was open I hightailed it. I went from 105 on the roof to 45–50 degrees in the butcher shop. My first day at the butcher shop was December 4, 1984. That was about twenty-seven years ago.

We had an old-time Italian butcher shop called Petrini Meat Market. We had 120-foot meat counter. We had beef in front and the whole veal and lamb, and we displayed it all on ice, really nice.

I started out as an apprentice butcher, first, second, third, fourth stage apprentice butcher. Then I was a journeyman, but I was already assistant manager when I was third stage apprentice. I was working out of the union hall as a journeyman and at other stores on my two days off. I was so greedy and I liked the money. I was getting journeyman wages by the time I was second stage apprentice—$20 an hour—and I'm supposed to only be making ten an hour. I was making $20 an hour on my days off too. If you came in early and took short lunches and stayed late and not on the clock, you'd get good hours, good shifts. But I did that for my own personal reason. I wanted to learn the whole business. I wanted to learn everybody's different ways on how to cut meat and then take the best of everybody. I was a good butcher; I am a good butcher.

My parents are great people. My dad is probably the most perfect guy I know, honestly I can say that. I've never heard him cuss, never seen him smoke, doesn't drink. He's just good people. Good-hearted people. When you're young, you think your mom and dad are the worst people. I remember my mom picking us up from school in her Volkswagen beetle with the music blaring. My mom likes to have fun—she's just a fun lady. She's a little on the wild side. My mom likes to do a lot of antique shopping. My dad doesn't like it, but he'll go and sit out on a park bench or whatever. They've been married since she was sixteen, I think.

My mom and dad weren't poor. I remember when my mom and dad had a Volkswagen beetle and another car I was embarrassed of. My mom and dad bought me a brand new motorcycle and man, that was neat. My mom and dad always took care of us.

My parents weren't missionaries but they did some missionary work. I guess you could call them part-time missionaries. My dad made plenty of money and he could take off for a year and go live someplace and do some missionary work.

Norm Van Brocklin, my uncle, was the star of the family and he died at a young age. He was a great quarterback and he holds the all-time passing record in the NFL. John Madden talks about him all the time. Have you seen the movie *Invincible*? At the end when he's giving that big speech in the locker room he talks about it being a great team and doing great things—and being like Norm Van Brocklin, the football player. But I never really got to know him. I was living in Missouri when I heard he passed away.

Ambassadors of the

When I met my wife Theresa I decided to come out here to Texas. I was twenty-eight when I met her and she was three years younger. Her mom and dad are Frank and Yvonne Webb. Her daddy works on oil wells in other countries. He was on CNN because he was over in Kuwait when problems started happening. He was at the Dead Sea during 9/11, drilling for oil when that happened. So he's been around a lot of stuff. Frank was a hard, hard worker. I have a lot of respect for hard-working people. Theresa was a hard-working young lady. She was the most hard-working one of the family kids.

Theresa ran a bridal shop. Her mom had a restaurant—this restaurant where we are sitting now doing this interview. The name of the restaurant is The Highlander Restaurant and it's been here since the late '60s. John Hoover and Jim Luther were two of the guys who built this place. John Hoover is a really nice guy and he runs the town. Super nice guy, nice friend—he could tell me about every piece of wood and where this came from.

Frank worked overseas, and when he came back he worked here like a mad man. He always warned me about the water in Burnet. "If I drink the water, and next thing I know my wife's having a baby."

Cole, my son, was raised in this restaurant.

This restaurant does better when the economy is at its worst. That is because you could probably eat here cheaper than you can at the grocery store. If you serve good quality food at a fair price people will keep coming back. Having a butcher shop here and us cutting our own meat is important. I brought the butcher shop here, but I actually bought all the equipment here. You've got to keep your costs down. There's no way you can serve the lunch you serve if you don't do the work yourself.

What would I like to say to the young people of today? When you are in school you need to pay attention and listen. When you get out in the world there will be many challenges and you have to have a strong desire to achieve something. I like my kids to try something. Just like the food—we tell our kids, "Try it, if you don't like it you don't have to eat it, but at least try it."

CASTROVILLE

Ambassadors of the

Bette Hamby

Castroville, Texas-Eureka, California

I was born in Eureka, California and raised in southern California at the Bell Flower area. My husband and I moved to Texas on December 31, 2003. We drove out of California on New Year's Eve 2003 and started our second part of life. I retired from my escrow career after thirty years and my husband retired from working for the State University in Fullerton after twenty-five-and-a-half years. Our two adult children both followed us.

I'm a sixth generation descendant of Castroville. My mother's ancestors helped establish Castroville so I had been coming to Castroville since I was a baby, just about every year, or sometimes a couple times a year, and sometimes not for a couple of years. We vacationed here from the time when I was a small child. Even after we got married, my husband knew this was a second place for us to visit. We never looked at it to be our home, it was just where we went to visit my family.

My mother was born and raised in San Antonio and met my father while he was in the Air Force. He was stationed in Lackland. His family was in Eureka, so when they married they moved to California and stayed there until about fifteen years ago. Then moved back to Texas. That's how I came along.

I didn't know that I was going to be glad to be back in Texas. We wanted to be here because our family was here. And we felt God was moving us here when we made the decision to come. About two or three months after we moved here, all of a sudden I realized that I felt like I'd had a part of my heart missing that I didn't realize was missing. Suddenly, there was this contentment that I didn't have before. But when I got here it seemed like everything was right, like this was supposed to be all along. Like I don't remember ever *not* being here, which I thought was very interesting.

We were in California from 1956 to 2003, about forty-seven years. That's where my husband and I met, married, and our children were born. It was fine and we enjoyed it and all our friends. We had a great church and lots of friends that we had made through the church. We have lots of wonderful memories. We had a wonderful beach that we loved going to. The recreation resources were plenty and they were all within a couple of hours driving time. We enjoyed everything about it. We really liked it except the cost of living was becoming so high that there was a big premium—stress included—for enjoying that life.

When I was a very young child I was probably an adventurer. I liked trying things, and even if I got hurt I wasn't smart enough to figure it out and I'd go back and try it a second time. And yes, I was one of the kids who put her tongue on a frozen ice tray and ran down the hill just to see what it was like. I tried all those things. I was the adventurer. I was my dad's "son" because he had no sons. I would be under the car with him making repairs.

Dad was a general contractor by trade and I went to work with him and helped him nail up Sheetrock. This was at a very young age, probably ten or eleven. I was never as good as his workers, but in my eyes I felt like I was doing a great job and it was all fun. When we had work we had the things we needed. When there was no work, we didn't. It was a family business and lots of times we had to help all the family members. We moved a lot. I went to quite a few of the schools in our city and I wasn't in any one place for long, maybe a couple years at a time.

When I was about seven through ten years of age, the Watts riots in Los Angeles were going on. There was a sense of fear—we lived about ten miles from where the riots were happening. At one home we lived in, Dad would go out first to check that everything was all clear before we could go outside. That was a sense of insecurity for them as well as for us because we didn't know what to expect.

During my teen years the riots had pretty much subsided and we were into the nice mid-sixties. The Beatles . . . the older generation, my parents' age at that time, didn't understand the Beatles. It was an interesting time of trying to help them understand rock music and all those types of things.

Ambassadors of the

I couldn't wait to get my driver's license—I was in the line the first minute I could get my permit and the first to get my license. After getting it, you couldn't hold me back. I called my girlfriends and we took my car and headed out to what was called Cherry Valley. We went to pick cherries on Saturdays, and we were pretty much on the wheel ever since.

As a teenager I had a number of responsibilities. I helped with taking care of the home because my mother was a stay-at-home mother until I was about thirteen. My dad was a general contractor working for himself and we didn't have insurance. He wanted to have insurance for my mother, my sister, and me and for himself because he was not well and had a lot of health issues. My mother went to work at JCPenney as a sales associate. When she went to work, we all pitched in and started helping. When she wasn't working in the daytime hours she did ironing for businesses. We used to joke that we had more clothes in the refrigerator than we did food. My dad worked a couple jobs and so for us it was just helping all of us get through.

I worked three jobs before I was sixteen, because that was instilled in me and I was a worker. I babysat and on the holidays I worked in a flower shop. I helped clean and sweep and do all the things in the flower shop. When I was a junior in high school I left at noon and worked in the elementary school as a student aide, and then babysat in the evenings. It was then that I decided I wanted to work when I was out of high school. I started working at a doctor's office for a group of physicians and still did the babysitting and worked at the flower shop as well.

School was good and I excelled in my studies. I enjoyed having the teachers tell me I was doing well. I always loved to read and I enjoyed my studies and got pretty much As and Bs. I didn't push myself in class. I should have, I could have, I could've done very well. I took basic math because I knew I could ace it. I tried algebra and decided I was never going to need that because all I was going to do was get married and have babies and live in a house with a white picket fence.

When I graduated and had no boyfriend, I figured that idea was probably not there. So I went to work. I had thought about going to law school and I decided not to. My father begged me to go to college, but I had the idea that I needed to make money because when we were growing up we didn't have any. I had one pair of shoes: black-and-white saddle oxfords. I wanted more shoes and more things. I wanted more of whatever it was and I knew I wouldn't have it unless I worked for it.

A friend of mine introduced me to the Soroptimist Club and I owe credit to it. Soroptimist is like a Rotary Club, a service-oriented group for women. If I didn't have the Soroptimist Club and this wonderful group of businesswomen who took this crazy teenager and instilled in me confidence and the ability to be in business I don't know if I would have the career I had. Those crazy ladies put up with a bunch of us teenagers from high school and loved us and taught us that it was okay for women to be in business.

One of the ladies called me up one day and said she wanted me to come work for her. I wanted just one job instead of three, so she invited me to work for her in the escrow business. That was August of 1974. I started at $2 an hour and I was thrilled to get it and work a full-time job. That led to what's now an almost thirty-seven-year career.

For fun I went on weekend trips with my girlfriends and we'd go to the park or the beach. My fun was not a lot but it wasn't limited either. I just enjoyed everything I was doing and I never looked at it as not having fun. I was not a party person so I stayed home. My sister enjoyed life as well, but I was more of a homebody and I really liked being with my family.

At this point, I regret not going to college. I feel that it would have given me maybe more credibility. I don't know that I know any less because of just having street knowledge or worldly knowledge, so to speak. But I think that in our economy today something about a college degree gives a person more credibility. Many people get their degrees and never use those degrees. But there's something about having that degree, from an employer's standpoint—they think you're more valuable. I would never instruct anybody not to get a degree in this day and age.

As a preteen, I first experienced death when my grandfather died. People around me had died, but I was pretty much shielded from it. First my grandfather died and then my grandmother died just a few days after my twelfth birthday. Those were sad times. My grandmother was the one who took me to church and first started me having a spiritual relationship with the Lord. She and I were very, very close and losing her was hard.

School life dealt hurts from friends—a sad time because I was not the most popular kid in school and I got the typical ridicule that kids go through. I felt disappointment that some kids got things we didn't because of our financial situation. Those were the normal things I think most people face. The hardest part was not being accepted more in high school, that was the biggest disappointment I had.

I started working in escrow in 1974 in California. In Texas it's known as title, but it's the same kind of work in both states. When somebody buys a house or sells a property, commercial or residential, typically you have a third party that is not interested in the property. It's non-bias and the escrow holder acts as a holder of funds and documents until a certain set of conditions have been met. That's what we do; we hold people's deposits and we hold sellers' deeds until they've complied with the terms of their contract. Then we give the seller the money and the buyer the deed and they go on. In the early years it was just done with a handshake. When the handshake subsided, people went into having somebody they could trust holding those documents.

Crystal, my daughter, has been working with me in this business since 1998—she's been my right hand for a long time. We both work this office and we're a branch office for Tom Rothe, who's an attorney and has two branches in Hondo and Castroville. We cover anyplace in Texas that we can do closings for. We're not necessarily licensed by issuing policies, but I have additional companies I can partner with and we can work through them. We're licensed by the state of Texas and only work in Texas.

Ambassadors of the

My parents are still alive and they are wonderful. I'm blessed to still have them with me. My dad just turned eighty. I get my sense of adventure and entrepreneurship from him. He's always ready to try something else—let's do this and what can we do for that? He was a product of the Depression and because of that, he has certain ideals, which are good ideals but difficult for some of today's generation to understand.

My mother was born in 1936, so she was just outside of the Depression era. She likes security and is a Texan through and through. She is caring and nurturing when it comes to making sure that we all feel like a great family. She's a great cook and I learned how to cook from her. She's tough and she knows how to work hard because she worked alongside my dad. They built the house we're in now and she helped dig trenches for their waterlines. She's a trooper. She's had to go through an awful lot. She's the oldest of nine kids and my dad was the middle of five kids. They're good people and they taught me about being a volunteer with the spirit of giving back and helping others.

Our home was always a place that our neighbors' kids came to—my mom and dad would say, "Bring your kids over here." They were friends' friends and still are. They actually helped save a marriage because of their wisdom and love for this couple. They're pretty cool.

My grandmother on my father's side was tough lady and strong as an ox. She'd pull a snail off a plant and step on it barefooted. It didn't bother her at all. She survived the Depression and lived in a tent on the beach in Bakersfield. They picked cotton and did whatever they could do to try to make ends meet. They put two or three tents together to try to make room for all of them. She was a true pioneer woman. In my eyes, she was just a phenomenal giant of a person.

My grandmother on my mother's side was born in Missouri. My grandfather was part of the Oklahoma Land Rush. My ancestors were German and French.

Traveling has been fun with the family, but limited. We loved to travel and started our kids traveling from the time they were small. Even if we didn't have money for big adventures or big vacations we always took a vacation, usually by car. I've been to most western states but I've never been to the eastern states other than Florida. Some day I want to do the East Coast. I went to Kauai, Hawaii after we moved here and I figured we'd never take any vacations again. I was blessed to be able to go to Kauai. I absolutely loved it. I also went to Arizona and New Mexico. We've camped out, gone fishing, been in the snow and on the river. We've only flown a few times with the kids, when they were little, most trips were with our car.

My daughter, Crystal, is single and she's a real help to me. She has a special touch and children love her. She's brilliant when it comes to numbers and she's detail-oriented. She has blessed the lives of a lot of people. My son, Aaron, is married and lives in California. Not long after we moved here he decided he wanted to be with his girlfriend and he ultimately married her. He has his own business there, an alloy business. His wife is an art teacher and she just received her master's degree. They blessed me with a "granddog" named Lizzy and she's a cutie. Both Aaron and Crystal are a lot of fun.

Probably the legacy I would like to leave my children is to never give up. There are a lot of bumps on the road in life, but don't let them stop you—just keep going at it. Be respectful and be kind to one another. Those are important things that I hope I've shown them in my life. I have tried to show them what it's like to turn the other cheek, so to speak, even when you're totally right in your way. The Bible says you should forgive one another seventy times seven. I hope my children see that we've tried to live that and given them a spiritual legacy; that's very important for us. Also, we hope they see that we want to give back.

We're all born with dreams in our hearts. God has given everybody a purpose and my dream is to help women discover what that purpose is. I'm a Life Purpose Coach. It means I work with women, asking them questions much like what you're asking me right now. I help them discover what God has planned for their lives. Many times people start out with dreams as children, and then life's bumps and rejections cause them to forget about their dreams. They end up somewhere along the road as older adults and never follow their dreams and they live with regrets. My goal is to help women sparkle from the inside out. And you do that when you are fulfilling and living the purpose God has for you.

Not long before we moved to California, I felt dead inside. I didn't have any life inside of me. I was just doing the routine things because that is what I learned to do, but I was not very happy. I met a lady who is a motivational speaker and a coach at a work conference and she did some training with me at one of her sessions. She called me back and explained the value of becoming a Life Purpose Coach. When she gave me that description, I just started sobbing because it fit me exactly. Through knowing her and attending some other sessions, I decided that what she did for me I wanted to do for others. I hired her as my coach about a year before we moved. I didn't know I was moving at that time, I hired her so I could be a better person at work. I was general manager and vice president and I was supervising twelve offices. I hired her so she could help me be a better ministry worker, a better homemaker, a better employee and employer. During that process God showed us we were supposed to move to Texas, so then she became a transition coach for me. She helped me to be able to let go of those things and move to Texas.

When I moved here I thought I had everything all figured out. Then about a year and a half after moving here, I suddenly hit the wall. I had no ministry to involve myself in, no career because I wasn't working. We really hadn't developed a friend base yet, so I had no friends, and we hadn't developed a church base, so no church. Both of my children had moved back to California, so suddenly all those things I valued were gone. That's when I heard about a ministry that was training women to become Life Purpose Coaches. I checked into it and they accepted me for the training—that was probably about June of 2005 and from that moment my life changed.

The training was incredible because it gave me a new sense of what I was supposed to be doing all along. I met some incredible women from around the world. Like I said, when we retired and moved here I figured my travels were done. I have traveled more since we moved here, through my coaching, and have met incredible women that I would never have met otherwise. Also, I had an opportunity to work with some exciting clients so it's been quite a reward for me. I have a cute little bottle on my desk that says "coach" on it. What I do in here helps make money but, more so, my passion is to be a Life Purpose Coach.

Although I work from my home, Life Purpose Coaching International is featured out of Orange County. We have coaches around the world now. The main book we use as a training premise has been translated into nine languages. We have a group going to South Africa this summer to help set up another center there.

If someone who reads this book is interested in the program they could contact me because I'm a licensed instructor. I've been certified to train and to instruct other women to become Life Purpose Coaches as well. I'd be happy to help them. The women I have met through coaching have been remarkable and their stories are just like my story. Their stories are inspiring and touching. They really do have dreams. You may not be where you want to be, and you may have to go out of state to figure it out, but don't let that stop you.

Jonathan D. Fish

Castroville, Texas-Riverside, California

I was born and raised in Riverside, California, which is about sixty miles outside of Los Angeles. My wife and I were looking to move out of California due to financial reasons and, unfortunately, because her mother had passed away. I had family here in Texas that we had recently reconnected with and they said, "Come out and visit, you'll love it." We didn't believe them, but we visited and fell in love with Castroville and San Antonio—and here we are today. We first came here for a three-day weekend, to explore and reconnect with our family, as well as to see different sights. We had never been to Texas. We didn't know

Ambassadors of the

what the area was like. When you go on Google, or any of the map systems, you can't get a sense of the people, the surroundings, or anything like that. My family drove us to San Antonio, and we started out towards Schertz and Cibolo as well as around San Antonio and Helotes. We went everywhere, looking at neighborhoods and seeing what we liked and didn't like.

We had a number of reasons for leaving California. The cost of living there is considerably higher than Texas. My wife was working full time and I was a stay-at-home dad for the two years before we moved here. I also had a business, working as a potter. Due to my wife's mother getting sick and various other reasons, I had to put my business on hold. We helped her mom and her dad for a while and it gave me a chance to connect with my son. I have no regrets. It was the most important decision I ever made in my life, to put my son first.

My son is going to be five in April. We had just gotten married and we had our son immediately after that. We knew her mom was sick with kidney failure and was on dialysis, and later we found out she had cancer. Even before we knew about the cancer, we knew if she was ever going to see her grandson we needed to do it now. She was able to spend six months with him and it was a blessing.

My childhood was pretty good. When I was between six and ten years old my parents separated and then divorced. It was difficult, I think, when it first came up, but I was easy to accept it because I didn't really understand what was going on. It definitely changed our lives, having to live in a different place, and go back and forth. But my parents were good parents, they loved us, they took care of us, they fed us, they clothed us.

I had a lot of friends. I went to a Catholic school, Queen of Angels in Riverside, and I participated in all kinds of sports, mostly T-ball when I was younger and later basketball and football into high school. School was good, but it was a little difficult at times. My parents were not Catholic, and I'm not Catholic, but I went to a Catholic school. However, I excelled in my studies and my education—even religion class. But not having that support at home sparked me to question more often than I probably should have, because I didn't understand where the teachers were coming from.

I was raised by a father who didn't believe anyone unless he could show proof, basically. And to a certain extent that has made me a better person, but it's also hindered me in being accepting of people because I want to see proof often. I have to stop myself and think about that. It's something I've been working on since I was a kid, trying to figure out who I am and how I'm going to treat people. Am I going to take them at face value or do I want to see more than one side? And I do want to see more of what's going on and see the truth behind people. I think to do that you have to take a chance with people, you have to trust them to a certain extent.

When I was young, my chores at home included taking care of the dog and everything that goes along with that. Also, taking out the trash and doing yard work. My teen years were pretty good, but pretty erratic. I moved in with my father when I was eleven. Eventually we moved in with one of his girlfriends, whom he is still with today, and their son Jason, who was one grade behind me in grade school. Jason and I were good friends.

My high school career was pretty crazy, pretty tumultuous, coming from a private Catholic school that was very conservative and then going to a public high school. It was kind of a rude awakening. People of all different colors, creeds, and everything else. It was very difficult my first two years to feel a part of something and not like an outsider.

My father is Clifford Edward Fish and my mother is Laura Ann Fish. I know my dad was born in upstate New York, in Glens Falls, I believe. When he was five years old, he and his family moved to Exeter in northern California where his family ran a resort. He spent a good portion of his younger years in northern California. They eventually moved through California and near Reno, Nevada and Tahoe. Currently my father's mother, Theresa, resides in Reno Sparks, Nevada.

My father, in his younger years, did all kinds of work but the main job that supported him and my family was with Pacific Bell. He was a telephone maintenance provider.

My mother, I believe, was born in North Carolina. I don't know exactly when they moved to southern California but her father, my grandfather Luther, was in the Marines. They moved onto the Marine base at Camp Pendleton. They lived there for a portion of her childhood, and at seventeen she got a job with Pacific Bell.

My career in pottery has had its ups and downs. I started out working out of the junior college. I wasn't happy with school because I felt like I was attending to appease my parents and everybody else. So I asked myself: What do I enjoy? What do I love doing? I realized that the only class I enjoyed was pottery and that's all I wanted to do. I decided to try and hone my skills and I started a pottery business. At the time, I was working, putting myself through school, and I didn't have the money to get started. My wife's parents were very supportive and they gave me a loan, under contract, of course, and they helped me buy my first kiln and get my business going. It was a dream come true for me. I purchased a kiln and some of the other equipment necessary—a potter's wheel and an extruder—and I asked my mother if I could convert the garage into a studio and hook up a kiln. She has always been so supportive of me and she said, "Of course."

I have been commissioned many times to make pieces. Recently I finished an order for a wedding party for mugs and tankards. I'm still getting established here in Texas but I've sold on the Internet, I've sold through consignments, and I've sold custom orders. Custom orders are the bulk of my business.

Making pottery has improved my relationship with my father. My father and I talk about each other's pottery, as well as different techniques, how to solve problems, and issues that we're having. It has definitely brought us closer. There was a time when I was not respectful to my father because I had lost all respect. I blamed him for things that happened between him and my mother. But the art, the pottery, wanting to explore new techniques and to have someone to

Ambassadors of the

share it with has brought us closer together. It has given us the common ground we needed. Growing up I wanted to think he was perfect or should have been perfect, but now that I'm a father I realize how difficult that is. It's awesome to share a love and a hobby that, when you're doing it, it takes all the pressures of the world away.

My wife, Christy, is the love of my life. And I have a beautiful son, Aiden Michael Fish, and they're the light of my world. Before I met my wife things weren't going so well. I had gone through a series of hardships—family, personal, and financial. I mean, you name it, and I got to a point where I felt like why me? Finally, after I dug myself out of the hole and focused on myself, there she was. When God put her in my life it changed my life completely. It really brought a new perspective. I knew on our second date I wanted to marry her—I didn't want to let this one go. We got married in 2005 and we had our son a little after and he's one more of the greatest gifts.

My son is amazing. In a lot of ways he has certain characteristics of mine, but he's smarter than I was at that age. He's inquisitive, he wants to know. I don't think I started asking the questions he asks until I was in high school. And he's a lot like my wife. When he talks to people they are the center of the conversation and his world at that time. He has a way of bringing joy to people.

I really believe that difficult family relationships can change us in a negative way or in a positive way. I've chosen to make it a positive in my own life, and in my family's life, and in my father's relationship with his grandson, my son. They have a wonderful relationship and it's spread through our whole lives.

For my son, the most important thing is that I love him, and I believe in a God that loves him. I want him to know that. I want him to have the strength and to know that even if there's a time in his life when he has to stand alone that there is someone who cares about him. That's the legacy I want to leave him. I don't care about being the best potter, or providing a big house. I'm going to be there for him and when I mess up I want to be able to tell him I'm sorry and say, "Hey, I messed up." That's something I never got as a kid. Don't look at me as perfect. And to the younger generation I'd like to say, we get caught up in this world with our things and our stuff and everything seems so important. But there are only a few things that are truly important: family, love, kindness,

Ester Calvert

Castroville, Texas–Chapin, Iowa

I want to be known as a good mother because I feel as if that is the one thing in which I succeeded.

Ambassadors of the

CENTER POINT

Silvia Konrad, Foreign Language Teacher/Restaurant Owner

Center Point, Texas-Rome, Italy

Be yourself, but also be open to accept others and everything that they are.

Ambassadors of the

CLEBURNE

Jeff Gottfried, Teacher/Sculptor

Cleburne, Texas–Tracy, California

For my son, I could only wish that I could give him as blessed an upbringing as I had. That would be a tall order in my eyes, and basically means being a good father. Stick with it, whatever it is. Be stable and follow your dream.

Ambassadors of the

COMFORT

Richard Holmberg

Comfort, Texas–Hinsdale, Illinois

I am originally from Illinois. I grew up and was educated in Illinois and then gradually moved further south until I wound up in Texas in 1970. Part of that was employer-induced, driven by my career with Exxon, but I always had a personal affection for Texas because I admired the independence of Texas, the people, the beauty and variation of the land. I prefer a warmer climate than I knew growing up in Illinois.

I worked for Exxon for thirty-three years. I worked in Illinois for a few years and then got transferred to Houston in 1970. We moved around the country,

Ambassadors of the

in and out of Houston, over those thirty-three years. Every time we came to Houston, we took little trips to explore different parts of the state. We used to go up to Lake Travis and from there take day trips to see different parts of the Hill Country. We kind of fell in love with the Hill Country.

We got to a stage when we felt we were not going to be moving around too much anymore, we were pretty well set in Houston for the rest of our careers. Then we decided it would be nice to have some property in the Hill Country. Over a five-year period, whenever we had a holiday weekend with nothing to do or some spare vacation time, we explored different parts of the Hill Country. We met with realtors and checked available properties and eventually found a property in Comfort that was exactly what we were looking for. It needed a little work because it was covered up with cedar and brush, but we thought it would work for us. We eventually bought this property in 1993.

My career with Exxon started out in marketing. I was in marketing for about five years; the rest of that thirty-three years was in human resources. I did human resource management in all different parts of Exxon, all over the country, but I've never lived outside the country. I worked in Exxon companies that did business outside the country. We had fourteen mailing addresses over those thirty-three years. We've already lived here longer than any place in our married lives.

I grew up, in my opinion, in a very desirable environment. We lived in the western suburbs of Chicago. My dad worked for Inman Steel Company in the city and he commuted by train. I went to school in the little town I grew up in, Hinsdale, Illinois. It had a good school system and great people. It was a small town when I lived there, surrounded by farms on all sides. Today, you couldn't separate it from the city. But, it was a very nice experience.

When I grew up, sports were very much a part of our lives—football, basketball, and baseball. I played Little League, football, basketball, and other sports activities. I always liked being with my dad when he played golf on vacation and went fishing a lot with him. My dad died when I was a freshman in college and that had a large impact on my life. He was sort of my model, if you will. I still admire him to this day and think a lot about him. But, I also had a lot of mentor teachers and coaches. My mother was important, obviously. We had a good time growing up. I have great admiration for both of my parents. They were very influential in my growing up years and continuing to this day. I also have an older sister who was very important to me—she still lives in that area.

High school was a good experience for me. I was involved in politics and became a class officer and president of my freshman and senior classes. I was very much involved in sports including track, football, and a little basketball. I had a lot of great friends and some of them continue to this day to be great friends. We were very happy, as most high school kids are, socially, athletically—I just enjoyed school.

I went to Northwestern University in Evanston, Illinois. I studied marketing and political science and received a degree in marketing. That's where I met my wife, Julie.

During my senior year I interviewed with several oil companies and was hired by Humble Oil and Mining Company. It became Exxon over time. Julie and I got married shortly after graduation and we both went to work. I went to work for Exxon and Julie was a schoolteacher.

Eventually we had two children, Dick Jr. and Ann. They were born in 1966 and '68 respectively. They are still very close to us to this day. Today all our children and grandchildren live in Austin.

My son manages a software group for Dell Computers in Round Rock. He enjoys his work a great deal. He graduated from Vanderbilt University and went to the University of Texas for his master's in electrical engineering. He then went into software engineering with another company in Atlanta and wound up with Dell.

My daughter and her husband are professional photographers. They had a studio on the west side of Houston called Tomorrow's Memories. They got tired of that business and sold it. They eventually went to Austin. My son-in-law, Tom, is currently working with an advertising, marketing, and printing company in Austin using his graphic arts and management skills. My daughter right now is a very good mom to my other grandson.

We have always enjoyed wine as consumers. We had taken trips to some of the wine regions of the world: the Bordeaux area, Tuscany in Italy, and Napa in California. On our first trip to Napa we sort of got the bug. We filed it away in the back of our minds that if we ever had the right property where we could grow grapes, it would be nice to have a small vineyard. When we bought our land in Comfort, it was really not for the intention of growing grapes, it was more a country and recreational property. After we acquired it, we thought, maybe we can grow grapes out here. So we had some experts look at the soil samples, and talked to some other people who were growing grapes in the Hill Country and running wineries. We got very involved with some of them. Danny Hernandez at Sister Creek has been especially helpful to us in understanding what's involved and getting us started. We were able to get a consultant to help us plant a vineyard.

In 1998 we planted the Merlot vineyard and it's about 2.5 acres, which is just a small vineyard. We started out selling grapes just like we had thought about. Singing Water Vineyards is our corporate name and the winery is Singing Water Winery.

It's been amazing with all this traffic, with people coming in for wine-tasting. We're kind of off the beaten path, way out here in the country, five miles south of Comfort. If people want to come here they can go to our website SingingWaterVineyards.com.

Most of our wine is sold right here in the winery. We do have eleven wholesale accounts. Those accounts are mostly small, one-of-a-kind restaurants here in the Hill Country and the small towns around us. A couple wine bars and package stores sell our wines.

The business has grown a little faster than we had anticipated and we're continuing to need more help to manage it. We recently had discussions with our

Ambassadors of the

daughter and son-in-law about coming to help us. There's a good possibly they will, sometime in the future, be joining us to help expand this business and make it part theirs.

It's much more than a full-time job right now and that's why we need more help. We have seven people part-time who help run the tasting room here and I have one full-time helper. We bring in volunteer grape pickers. We have some very labor-intensive activity in the vineyard a couple times a year. We have our harvest days and we have a group of wonderful friends and neighbors who like to help us pick grapes and help us to celebrate harvest. These people will work for wine. They pick grapes and we give them a bottle of wine.

Harvest season is usually a couple of weeks. We get all the grapes in during this time and then do the crushing, the fermentation, and the pressing. The red wines go into oak barrels for the long process of barrel-aging.

Some wineries still have people stomp the grapes with their feet. I have actually offered to get the old tub out for some of my pickers. But, usually they prefer to watch the automatic crusher. Some people like to get their feet nice and red. Some of the wineries even provide you with a T-shirt you can step on when you have grape juice on your feet to make the imprint and they have the winery's name at the top.

At the end of harvest, about week later, we have a harvest party. Everyone who participated in that year's harvest is invited to come celebrate with us. We have a little music, food stations around the winery, and the tasting room is open. We just have a good time.

What kind of legacy would I like to leave my children, grandchildren, and the young people of today? I would probably need to give that a lot of thought to be complete about it, but the importance of faith and family would be at the top of my list. I think faith in God is a wonderful thing and it gets you through the hard times. It also helps you appreciate the good times and keeps things in perspective. I think family is extremely important. One of the things I'm really concerned about in this country now is the family unit, which seems to be not as strong as it once was. We have a wonderful family and I hope it always stays that way. I have great kids, great parents, a wonderful sister, and wonderful grandkids. We try to work very hard at maintaining the tradition of family and the importance of family by being supportive and caring for others.

I think the other thing is putting something back into the community that has supported you. There are always people in need, and if you have the ability to help others, you have the obligation to do it. I think that's one of the more satisfying things we have done on occasion, when we had been able to do things to help other people. And I think also the principle that fairness, honesty, and hard work pays off is important.

Nicole Welch, Massage Therapist

Comfort, Texas–New York Mills, Minnesota

If you are able to help people, you should do it. Sometimes, if you just give people a smile, that can make their day.

DRIPPING SPRINGS

Thomas Glass

Dripping Springs, Texas–Oakland California

I was born in Oakland, California, but at about the age of six months we moved to Mule Shoe, Texas, so I was raised in a small town in the Panhandle. We had a very simple life. It was in the 1950s, a time when you didn't have to lock your door. You could run around the neighborhood and your parents didn't worry that someone was going to steal you and take you off to another state.

School was probably difficult for me, looking back now. My wife is an educational diagnostician, and I realize I probably had a little ADD. So it was hard for me to focus. I was a daydreamer in school. My first grade teacher didn't seem to like me very much. I remember her slapping me on the back in the water line, and that gave me a very bad impression of my first year. I got blamed for knocking a girl into the flowerbed when it was filled with water because I was nonchalantly walking out on the playground, swinging my arms, and knocked her into the water. I got in trouble and didn't know why I was getting in trouble. I didn't go to kindergarten and wasn't read to a lot, so I wasn't a very good reader and I fell into a low reading group. School was a little intimidating for me. I never really was a good student. I did like math and science—they were more my forte. And I was usually good in spelling.

In my early teenage years I felt like I looked awkward. I felt I was a little bit fat. I was beginning to like girls, but I was very shy. I continued to be shy through high school and had very low self-esteem. I didn't have a lot of confidence until I was seventeen years old and we moved from Mule Shoe to El Paso, Texas. When we moved to El Paso, I just instantly became Mr. Popular because I was from Texas and had this Texas drawl. The people from El Paso liked that. It was a big ego boost for me and a confidence-builder. From seventeen to nineteen I was a social person. I became very interested in girls and very confident. I dated a lot, had a lot of fun going to Eastwood High School in El Paso. Eastwood was a lot harder academically and I graduated from there in 1972.

I worked all through high school. During the summers I went back to Mule Shoe where my granddad had a farm outside of Mule Shoe. It's actually called Needmore. I worked on the farm until my senior year. In my senior year I went to work at a Phillips 66 service station. I was working fifty hours a week that year. It wasn't too smart a thing to do, but I like to make money.

Basically, my only chore at home was to take out the trash. I was just kind of "there" with my parents. The only rule was that I had to be in early. I thought I had to be in too early, so I would sneak out the window. These are maybe things you don't want to tell the kids. I would start my car up and go back out. I would come back in around midnight or one, and then sneak back in the house. The danger of growing up in El Paso was that we had Juarez right across the border. We would go over to Juarez and hang out. That would be very dangerous these days. We probably could have gotten into some pretty big trouble, but I was lucky. The Lord looked after me, I guess.

In high school, I played football for a short time through my freshman year. I played baseball in high school. I played Little League in Mule Shoe. We didn't have baseball in school in Mule Shoe, we had outside leagues. But in El Paso, I played baseball my junior and senior years. I didn't ever really excel in baseball. My dad played professional baseball, a left-handed pitcher named Don Moore. He got recruited for the Texas to Mexico League. He ended up playing for the Clovis Pioneers.

After I graduated from high school my dad expected me to go to college. The only two colleges I knew were West Texas State in Canyon, Texas, which is now West Texas A&M, and Texas Tech University in Lubbock. My grades weren't that great, and I didn't think I could get into Texas Tech. The SAT exam was very tough for me. I wasn't a test-taker, so I ended up talking my way into West Texas A&M.

I liked to socialize. I was in a fraternity, the social chairman in the college. In college I had a lot of fun and met a lot of people. Some of the best years of my life! I played intramurals and found out I was a pretty good wrestler in intramural wrestling—I got second in wrestling. That's pretty much all I did sports-wise. It took me five years to graduate. I did graduate, even though my grades weren't that great. My degree was in Industrial Distribution Business, half industrial courses and half business courses.

My parents met when my dad went to the concession stand and stepped on my mom's foot with his cleats. My mom was from Mule Shoe. They ended up dating and getting married. My mom had two brothers. One was named Wilcy Moore, and that's where I got my middle name. He was named after my great uncle. They were all professional baseball players.

My great uncle, Wilcy Moore, played for the New York Yankees. My maternal granddad was named Nudie Moore, and they both went to St. Petersburg, Florida to the New York training camp. My great uncle actually made the team and played for the 1926 Yankees. He became, of course, good friends with Babe Ruth. He played with Babe Ruth, Lou Gehrig, and Ty Cobb. Babe Ruth liked to drink a lot, and my uncle was a pretty honest guy, so "The Babe" always let him hold his money when he was going out drinking. Babe Ruth bet my uncle $300 that he wouldn't be able to get three hits all year. My uncle won the bet and Babe Ruth had to pay up.

I have worked a lot of my life and done a lot of different jobs. When I got out of college, I went to work for World Book and ChildCraft. My dad was with them and did pretty well. I went from World Book into the Texaco refinery and I worked as an operator for Texaco for five years. I went from the refinery into the insurance and investment business. I got my securities license and I can sell mutual funds. When I got my insurance license I started selling life insurance. I did that from 1984 until 2005. I was in Amarillo, and I became an independent agent. That is what I really enjoyed most, being an independent agent. I just did my own thing and won a lot of trips to a lot of different places. I've been to Cabo San Lucas, Mexico, to Maui, Hawaii, to Sidney, Australia, and Port Arthur, Australia. I've been to Vienna, Paris, and Salzburg and I've been on a Caribbean cruise. I won a trip where I could go anywhere in the world, but I chose New York City because I had never really spent any time in New York, I had just flown in and out of it.

One of my goals was to get more into the securities industry. In 2005, I went from the insurance base into the securities business. I finally found out that I actually could study and pass tests. I went to work with Edward Jones and worked with them for about two years, then got recruited to Smith Barney and I thought, *now I have arrived*. I had an office on Congress Avenue in Austin, Texas, right down from the capitol. All to find out I didn't like corporate America. And

Ambassadors of the

so I just decided to quit. I'm at an age where I don't want to be unhappy with whatever I'm doing, even if I have to make less money. Now I've gone into the home repair and remodeling business, something I've always loved to do. I always did it on the side, even when I was in the insurance business and working at Texaco. So I decided I'd do it for a living. That was a year ago and I really enjoy it.

When we came to Dripping Springs, one of the first things I did was get involved in the community. I did that through joining the Dripping Springs Rotary Club. I also joined the Chamber of Commerce, and then we opened a business in Dripping Springs. We contributed pretty heavily to the economy, and we had ten employees that we kept regularly going for us at our business. The Rotary has been very much of an inspiration to me. After only being there a little over a year, I was asked to be president and I took on that role. I had to take a leave of absence after nine months, but I came back and told them I'd be president again if they wanted me. I ended up serving as president the second time and finished that year out.

I think if you will practice the Rotary's Four Way Test in your business and in everything you do you'll be more successful. In all the things we think, say or do, we should ask ourselves: 1.) Is it the truth? 2.) Is it fair to all concerned? 3.) Will it build good will and better friendships? 4.) Will it be beneficial to all concerned? I think you've got to have a lot of integrity in your business dealings with people.

Michele Hoggart, Painter/Sculptor

Dripping Springs, Texas–New Bedford, Massachusetts

Work hard and you will reap the rewards. Look out for your parents and take care of them.

Qi Hoggatt

Dripping Springs, Texas–Urunqi, Xianjiang Province, China

People always call me Chi Chi. I live in Kyle, Texas, however, I work in Dripping Springs doing office administration, accounting, shipping, laser machine operation, and bookkeeping. I was born in Urunqi, Xianjiang Province, which is in the northeast of China, near Russia. When I was a child, my life was pretty happy and maybe a little bit stressful because I had to do something that my classmate friends did not do, and that was to go to English class every night after school. My dad asked me if I wanted to, he did not force me, and I said, "Okay, why not?" I started when I was four years old and I kept doing it for seven years. Now in China, children start learning English in kindergarten using simple words. Most of us started English at the middle school.

The conditions were pretty good because the city where I lived is the capital city, which is very pretty. I think my life was pretty lucky. I didn't have to worry about some things like my friends whose families had some difficult living conditions because their parents didn't have good jobs. I didn't have to worry about anything. My parents were able to provide for my needs, but during the weekend I had to clean the house.

I am the only child. China still has a policy of only one child per family. Yes, it is true, but at our age if we got married and we are both the only child in our families we could have two kids.

My teenage years were all about school and it was really stressful because you have to prepare for the test to go to the university. China has so many people that the competition is really hard. One out of ten applicants is allowed to go to the university—that is terrible. You go to school every day and have a lot of homework to finish and after midnight you go to sleep. During the weekend you maybe study some more in the areas you need to improve yourself. It was important for everyone to study all the time because it was and is the culture of our country.

I had a lot of friends and hung out with them during summer and winter vacations. We went to different places as a group of teenagers. We went to Xian as well as Hong Kong and Macao. I really enjoyed traveling—it was lots of fun.

After high school I went to the university in my own town where I majored in accounting. After I graduated it was a little hard to find a job, so I decided to go abroad to study and I went to Vancouver, Canada. I stayed there about eight months studying for my MBA, but did not finish because the program was for three years. I made a lot of friends while I was there.

My godmother lived in Texas where she owned a Chinese restaurant in Dripping Springs. I came here during spring break for a week, in 2008, to visit her and met my husband at the restaurant. At that time he was in college and worked in the restaurant as a waiter. It's a funny story. One night he asked for a take-out order when it was near closing time. He asked the owner if she spoke Mandarin or Cantonese. At that time he was studying Mandarin as his hobby. The owner asked him to work there. That is how we met. I asked her if he could speak Chinese. She said, "Yes, and that is why he works here."

We have been married for three years this month, June 24. We got married in Dripping Springs. We had a wedding party in China. My parents were here and they just went back.

My parents are very good parents. They both are very kind and they do many things for me. They think a lot for me. They both have pretty good jobs. My mom is an accountant and works at China Tobacco. My dad is a business manager for the China Coal Company. We use coal as our energy source. They

Ambassadors of the

are not like other Chinese people who force you to do this and tell you this way is right. Instead they say I should compare the different ways of doing things and decide for myself which way I should go. They will tell me if it is good or not good.

My grandparents on my mom's side are wonderful. I'm pretty close to them because my grandparents on my dad's side have passed away. Sometimes, we went to the grandparents' house every weekend to eat with them. They are so happy to see us. All the grandkids came back and we cooked together and we worked hard together.

My husband and I both like to travel and we will travel around in the future. Maybe I will work here or I will have another job, and maybe have a kid. In China, they prefer to have a boy to help do the farming. But it is okay to have a boy in the city, too.

I have learned a great deal about art and the people. People in Texas are pretty polite as well as very friendly. I learned a lot about art, crafts, and sculpture from my mother-in-law. She taught me how to do a design for a customer and to do a layout.

I think my life is a little bit different than many of my friends'. I have always trusted my parents. They tell me something because they have more experience and I trust them to help. For example, if they said I should go left and I think I should go right, I will consider their suggestion and then compare both sides. I think that helps me make good decisions. Young people should trust their parents. They should not ignore them or their suggestions and think they may be boring.

I am happy with my life. You can't ask for too much. You always compare yourself with people who are not as good as you or with people who are better than you. Everybody has one lifetime. Life is hard so you have to be happy.

Shigeru Nemoto, Stone Carver

Dripping Springs, Texas–Tokyo, Japan

Be a good human being and be a moral person. Study hard and go out and have fun.

Ambassadors of the

FREDERICKSBURG

Johann Eyfells

Fredericksburg, Texas–Reykjavik, Iceland

I was born and raised in Reykjavik, the capital of Iceland. It was a pretty small town with a population of about 30,000 when I was young. It's probably over 100,000 people today. In a little city, everybody seemed to know each other. It had a kind of intimate background. Iceland, of course, is a country that forms

Ambassadors of the

people. There is harshness and delight because the country is sometimes very harsh, cold, and forbidding and sometimes very nice, warm, and friendly.

I live now on ten acres of very beautiful land in Texas, close to Fredericksburg. I bought a ranch in Texas about seven years ago after living in Florida for a number of years. My wife died eight years ago. I lived at that time in Florida. Everything seemed empty and very much was missing. It created a hole, an emptiness in my life. Friends in Texas sent me pictures of this place. I was very much impressed with the eight buildings on ten acres of land. So I decided on the spur of the moment to send $50,000 to the banker and asked the banker to close the deal.

I think Texas is wonderful. There is an enough variety in the weather to look forward to different seasons. I like the sunny part best and the warm climate. I'm a sculptor and I do most of my work outside, so Texas is kind of an ideal place to work.

I vaguely remember my early life. I hardly ever dwell on the past. I'm an artist and a man of the future. I feel the future is infinitely more important than the past. I'm someone who might be called a futurist. Of course, you use the past as a springboard, as someplace to take off into the future.

My earliest experience in life that I can recall was probably when I was three or four. I was born in 1923 and this was probably in '26 or '27. I was on my grandfather's farm—he was a minister at that time. I was doing something a little bit nasty. I was catching some flies. I don't know what they are called in English, but we called them randa flies. They're pretty big flies and I buried them in the sand. I marked the grave, and every morning they were gone. They had gotten themselves out. I recall this as a tendency to investigate. I'm an investigator. I feel it is a little story that is indicative of what my nature is, which is to wonder what becomes of things. If I buried these creatures gently in the sand I was sure they would fly away. Soon enough they all did. They all got out.

I was pretty active as a teenager, especially in sports. Skiing was a major sport in those days for me. This was still in the Depression time. I remember my first skis. They were very elementary and totally improvised. I think I wore skis by the time I could walk. That's what I remember, skiing and walking came together in the same time span. I became a very good skier and was a specialist in slaloms. I became a champion of my town in the early 1940s. Although I received many medals, my mother always picked them up and I never knew what became of them. She was not one to flaunt things and I was not supposed to flaunt my medals. My teenage years were basically fun with sports and things of that sort.

I graduated from high school in 1941. I was thinking about going someplace to study at a university. I went to Berkeley, California to study in '45. I studied business in the beginning and then I transferred to architecture. I did a few years in architecture in Berkeley in the '40s. In 1949 I got married and took off for Florida, and that's where I got my degree in architecture. I worked on Long Island and in New Jersey. Also, I worked as an architect and a draftsman in New York.

I concentrated very seriously on art in the early '60s. I went back to school to study in 1960. I intended to earn a master's degree in architecture, but that didn't work out because I got into a disagreement with the professor. I wanted to do columns like tree forms and he wanted something more structurally sound. So, we didn't get along. There was a program in sculpture at the University of Florida. The professor of sculpture knew I was a good sculptor and he said, "Why don't you switch your major?" I got into the master's program in sculpture in the early 1960s. From there on, of course, it was all art in my book.

It was not my intention to teach sculpture because I was not a teacher. I did teach skiing as a young man, but I didn't like it very much because I'm not really a good teacher, I don't think. There was an opening for a teaching assistant at the University of Florida in Gainesville because a graduate student transferred to another school and she offered me her job. That's how I got into teaching in '62. I taught just design, elementary design, beginning design, and finishing design at the University of Florida in Gainesville.

From the beginning, most of my sculpture pieces were metal, especially aluminum. I'm still sculpting and I'm still working basically in aluminum. It became my calling. I felt it was a lucky break for me that the professor of sculpture somehow sensed I had a strong talent in sculpting.

I do not sell any of my art. Selling is the only thing that is somewhat disappointing. There are really no sales. Times are bad. I've never sold enough to call it a career. I've always had to teach. My art is my hobby and my life work.

I do exhibit my works. In fact, I exhibit all over the world. The major place is Biennale in Venice. Every two years there is an international show in Venice where every country, or almost every country, in the world has an exhibiting artist, and I represented Iceland in 1993. There are sculptures of all sizes, including paperweights and jewelry. Also, there are gigantic sculptures—the heaviest one is thirty-five tons. It is located right here, it's in parts right here. I moved it to here and I had to break it up.

I've exhibited all over northern Europe as well as in all the Scandinavian countries. Also in England, and there's a piece of mine in Hanover, Germany. The town bought a piece of mine in '66. I exhibited in Dubai, Emirates, for about three weeks and I participated in an international show in the Emirates in '95. I exhibited in a millennium celebration at the United Nations in 2000, where I was one of the international artists. So I have many good, strong exhibitions.

My parents were interesting people. My father was a landscape painter. My mother was a businesswoman who ran an embroidery shop for finery for female clothing and such. Actually, I was never too sure about my father's career in those days, in the 1920s, when I was speculating about the future. I felt he should go to work like everybody else at a regular job, but he was born to be a painter. No question about it.

They were very strict and quite religious. My mother was the daughter of a minister and as far as I know my father knew the Bible by heart. He was an avid reader of the Bible. They had honesty and integrity, and in every way exemplary behavior of human beings. They had a lot of influence on me. They were probably overly concerned with what I call "there's no free lunch." You have to earn a living.

I had one brother and two sisters. My brother died about ten or fifteen years ago. He was the eldest in the family. A sister died about ten years ago also. So there are two of us left, my younger sister and myself. She lives in Reykjavik, Iceland.

My wife Christin and I did not have children. The artworks are our children. I had a son out of wedlock when I was young and he is an engineer in Iceland. He is probably sixty-four years old and is a very active fellow.

The last time I was in Iceland was about six years ago. I was putting up a sculpture piece in my grandfather's churchyard. A very nice piece and it fits well in the churchyard. That was sort of a monument to his, or to my family's residence.

I have found Texas a fascinating place to live. Texas has always had a reputation for being an interesting, large, and demanding place. I think I picked the best place in America. These people are not buying sculptures, but in every other way this is an ideal place for me. I find there is a friendliness in the air.

My wife was almost the opposite of her self-portraits, which are very solemn. She was a very joyous person who was born and raised in Iceland. She painted her self-portraits as a depiction of a very strict, almost tyrannical personality, and I think she wanted to express seriousness to the world. That's her ability to dominate, her ability to call the shots, her ability to really accomplish the way she wanted those paintings to look. All her paintings have that determination that comes from her personality.

She has done about 500 in all. She has at least 250 to 300 oversized portraits. Lots of them are four by four feet, or four by five, or four by six. I try to do three exhibits a year of her work. What you see here is a small sampling of her best work. She has about 120 paintings of famous faces, too. This is a mixture of famous people and unknowns. She always had a studio where we lived in Florida.

I have written some essays in notebooks. I have written some short pieces of a philosophical nature that haven't been published, but there is a chance that some of this may be published later. There's some talk about putting it together into book form.

My legacy? It's to take matters into your own hands, to determine your way of life, by your own judgment and your own character. Of course, you follow a lot of rules that society hands you. You certainly try to become a good citizen. Use disappointments as springboards rather than as downers. Find a way of tapping into the energy of tragedy, the energy of disasters, and turn them into something great or totally valid. My wife and I did things our ways and we are leaving a large body of work that is representative of who we are.

Sherryl Brown

Fredericksburg, Texas–Bakersfield, California

I was born in Bakersfield, California in 1941 and lived there until I was six and a half years old. My early years were the war years, so it was a difficult time. My father was in the U.S. Navy. I think in 1942 he was drafted and he went to sea. My mother had three children by that time; I was the third one. Because it was a difficult time financially for my family we had to move in with my grandmother and grandfather in Bakersfield. My mother worked in Metro Field, which was a U.S. Army facility right outside Bakersfield, as a reporter. So I was at home with my grandmother from the time I was born until I was in kindergarten.

When my dad came back from the war he had a lot of psychological problems. He was discharged from the Navy because of a combination of drinking and psychological problems. I can remember my mother being quite unhappy during those years. My father went to work as an oil tool salesman for Tool, which is a Texas company, and we moved to New Orleans, Louisiana in 1946. It was a tremendous upheaval for my family. I was in kindergarten at the time so I made the adjustment fairly well. But I don't think my mother, my brother, or my older sister did as well as I did, moving to a whole new environment.

My father was struggling with alcoholism. It was a difficult time for my mother, because she was definitely a California girl. New Orleans is probably the largest departure anyone can imagine in the United States for a girl who grew up in Long Beach, California. My mother was pretty unhappy most of her life because of the displacement, the economic circumstances, and the disappointments in her marriage.

I'm very candid about my family. My mother and father should have had a wonderful marriage and their life should've been star struck. But because of the war, and alcoholism, and a number of other unfortunate circumstances, the marriage was not a good one. Everything that happened with my brothers and sisters was negative as a result of that poor beginning. There are seven of us and my six siblings have all had mental and emotional problems. I mean seriously, it's uncanny. I am the only one who lucked out and somehow got through the maze and managed to emerge intact. I can go through this world without being angry and accusatory and disturbed.

My teenage years were quite a bit better for me. I was somehow able to make an adjustment when my family moved from New Orleans back to Weatherford, Texas and then back to New Orleans again. By the time I graduated from high school, I had been in New Orleans a total of eight years. I made friends and I was lucky I got in with a group of YWCA leaders who helped us form a teenage club, kind of like a boys' and girls' club. It was a very community-oriented, nonprofit organization that gave me a lot of leadership experiences. I liked my school, I seemed to do well. I wasn't an A student but I made my grades. I did have a really good junior high school/high school experience; those were probably some of my better years as a child.

I graduated from Berlin High School in New Orleans, on the other side of the Mississippi River. I never dreamed of going to college, but after high school, I went to LSU miraculously. There were seven children in my family. I was the third, four more boys after me, so my mother and father were not able to send me to school.

Luckily, the National Defense Act came through in 1958 and I was able to get a loan from the federal government to go to college. I took advantage of that. I also had a job. I changed light bulbs in the dormitories for four years. That gave me additional income, plus I had a few small scholarships, but I was lucky, lucky, lucky to get to go to college. I knew it was my one opportunity and so when I got to LSU in 1959 I really hunkered down and I took it seriously. Somehow I made my grades and I found my wings. I majored in secondary education and graduated in 1963, in four years.

Health and physical education was my primary academic focus, but I specialized in health education. I did not want to coach because in my day girls didn't have any kind of athletic experiences through their schools. Luckily, my aunt taught me how to play tennis and I had experience in some sports. But I didn't feel comfortable in the athletic competitive domain. My entire career I refused to coach. First of all, philosophically, I had never really believed in athletics and the good that they can do for our children. Second, I'm not a competitive person, sports-wise. I don't think it brings out the best in us. I wanted to teach health education so that I could help people, especially my students, live healthier lives, learn how to eat properly, learn how to take care of their bodies. Especially mental health—because of my father I was always interested in mental health.

It was a good career, it was excellent. I went back to California after I graduated from LSU and I taught in Monterrey. I had a wonderful start to my career, overall. A lot of teachers tell me it was a terrible start for them. But when I had a principal that didn't support the teachers, I moved right away. And I kept going to school. I got two master's degrees during my thirties and forties. By going to school and moving about, I bettered my teaching circumstances. And I became a better teacher through having made those changes.

I have a master's degree in German and I have a master's degree in health education. I taught German at Austin Community College and at the University of Houston. I taught some in continuing education, but mostly at Austin Community College. That was my teaching assignment. After I retired in 1998 from Austin Community College, I took a job as executive director of the German-Texas Heritage Society. It is a statewide German Texan organization headquartered in Austin. That was a two-year position and I enjoyed it very much.

I came to Fredericksburg when I finished my teaching career at Austin Community College. Early on I decided I wanted to move to the Texas Hill Country and the opportunity came to buy a piece of property here. I moved and built a home in 2001. It was a conscious decision and a lot of research went into it. I tried to think of lifestyle, my interests, all the aspects of living in a more rural community. But it suits me fine and I found that I've got everything I had in Austin and more, living here in Fredericksburg.

I have lots of hobbies. I love to read, I'm an avid reader. I play golf. I'm physically active. I ride bikes, I swim. I'm teaching myself piano right now—I've always loved music. I played guitar when I was young. I love folk music, so I knew the whole Joan Baez songbook by heart. My cousin and I both shared that interest. I love to walk. I belong to the American Volkssport Association and like noncompetitive walking. I think it's fabulous. I do the crossword puzzle every day, which I think is fun, and I play Scrabble.

And, of course, my work with Johann Eyfells, the internationally known sculptor, is where I've committed myself. Until he dies, I'm going to be out there working with Johann. I just think he's one of the most remarkable men I've ever met and that's my commitment.

I lived in Germany for a period of time in my adult life. I wasn't happy with my teaching because I didn't think I was being effective. So I quit teaching and went to Germany. My goal was to stay a year, to study the language, and to work and to use my talents and skills. I was able to do that to a certain extent, but I wasn't able to really master the language in a year. I was in several small towns

Ambassadors of the

as well as Berlin and Hamburg. I taught in a small town that was beautiful, but it was in the British Zone and there were no American military personnel in that area.

I went on three different trips. I took a freighter from New Orleans, Louisiana by myself at twenty-three years of age and I went to Germany by myself. I knew I needed to grow up in many ways, and I needed to challenge myself in ways I hadn't been challenged.

My legacy to the young people of today—especially to my extended family of about thirty-eight people—would be a very simple one. There are some things that have helped me over my lifetime and they came from wisdom born of experience. I would tell them first of all to leave an example. I would like to think that I have had a positive experience on most of those people, all of those people—at least that I had something to offer them in terms of helping them to get where they wanted to go. I would like young people to realize we need to miss more things in life for in missing things we can be more contemplative. Being contemplative will lead us to a deeper understanding of the value of life and hopefully lead to maturity, so that when we make decisions they will be informed decisions—not those born of ego, or born of some naïve idea that we have to be famous, wealthy or beautiful. I think we have superficiality on that level, and that is frightening.

HARPER

Ambassadors of the

Diana Chaney

Harper, Texas–San Cristóbal, Venezuela

My husband, David, is from Texas, and as the saying goes, you can take a Texan out of Texas, but you cannot take Texas out of a Texan. His dream was to retire, which he doesn't like to call it, and become a rancher. We lived temporarily in Kerrville while building a house, a hacienda-style Venezuelan–Mexican house, in Harper.

My husband had a friend who retired from his job in Houston and became a real estate agent in Kerrville. David asked him to help us look for land to have our ranch and build our hacienda, which is called Doña Bárbara, my mother's name. Doña is a title you give to a Spanish lady, like Lord in English for a man. We are building a chapel on the ranch called St. Bárbara, which is one of the virgins we honor in Venezuela. Mainly we want to have this big house and relax, and wait until my daughter gets married and visits me with all her children.

When I was a little girl, life was free—totally free. I was raised on a farm that my mother had, that produced sugarcane and coffee. We were twelve children, nine girls and three boys. We had a teacher in the house on the farm that mother hired so the people in the village could learn how to read and write. We learned from this lady, too. We played a lot on the farm, too. I rode horses when I was a little girl. I'm hoping that I'll be able to ride again because I will try anything in life, again.

When I was a teenager, we moved to Tariba, to a house my mother inherited from her parents. It was a big, beautiful house with patios. My dream house in Texas is designed from that house. It is a little bit different because we cannot have the quarters and the patios that we had there because of the weather changes in the United States. We moved from Tariba to San Cristóbal and lived there until I was fourteen. It's ten minutes by car from Tariba, and that's where my father built a house.

When I was in San Cristóbal, I started to have my friends and a social life, and I went to the clubs. I went to Caracas because most of my older brothers and sisters went to the university and we wanted to be together. We moved to Caracas and it was really hard for me—even though I had eight sisters behind me, watching me—because I was the black sheep of the family. I was the one that wanted to go out to do things and always be happy.

At the age of twenty-three, I went to Boston to attend Boston University. The idea was to go there for a year to learn to speak English. Then I thought I would come back to Venezuela. While I was in Boston, I learned that being a student was beautiful again. It made me feel eighteen years old again. I took a test to go into the university and I had a high rank. That gave me an incentive. If I can do this it means my English is good enough, so I'm going to continue to study.

I couldn't handle the weather in Boston—too cold. And I was very lonely there. I never went out, I never enjoyed the city because I was depressed and alone, and because of the weather. I have a sister in Miami, and since I didn't have enough money to continue in Boston, I went to her house. Gladys, my sister, and her husband, Miguel, helped me a lot. I did some more courses in English and took accounting courses, to see what I was capable of.

Later I went to Lynchburg, Virginia. Unfortunately when I was there I had a car accident. My car skidded on an icy spot, and I lost control and went into a creek, forty-five feet. I had a couple fractures in my body and I had to interrupt my schooling. I went again to Miami to sister Gladys for help, and there my mother met me. Instead of going back to Venezuela, I stayed in Miami to recover from my injuries. When I was healed and able to do great at walking, I went back to Virginia just to finish the semester, then down to Miami again.

When you graduate, in Venezuela, as a Latin, you go back to the family. So I went back to my parents' home. Half of my sisters and brothers were already married. I lived with my mother and my father, and I started to work for a bank, Banco Latino. I started, like everybody else, in sales. I worked in sales for about a year or two, and I paid my novice (my dues). Then I went into commercial banking as the vice president of commercial banking.

When I was at the bank, I kind of got tired, I felt like I had a ceiling and I couldn't move forward. It was hard for me because banking wasn't exactly my vocation. I liked this area because it had a lot to do with people. I didn't have to be in the office eight hours. Most of the time we were out looking for clients. One day I found a list of suppliers and wholesalers for the petroleum company. They supply the petroleum areas with everything from valves to equipment and chemicals. These were large corporations or international companies, companies that were worth millions of Venezuelan dollars. So I started browsing this list and checking them.

I was able to find a job in the area of petroleum and chemicals, because I knew a little about it. I received support from many people. My boss at that time gave me support, too, so I got promoted. I started with my sales skills and worked with these companies. The vice president of the petroleum and chemical industries had a big petroleum show and all the multinationals, corporations, and medium-sized companies participated. Since I was with these companies I had the opportunity to go there, too.

I worked the first petroleum show and there I met my future husband. He went to Venezuela to open a company, but the main office was in Houston. The company he was working with before he went to Venezuela was Puffer-Sweiven. Puffer-Sweiven asked David to go to Venezuela to open a company there named Conind de Venezuela. I had that company on my list to open an account so we could make deposits from the money that we had and for the services they gave to the petroleum companies. Conind de Venezuela was a potential client for Banco Latino.

I had to coordinate all the business and all the interviews and the work that I had to do for the Banco Latino exhibit. I met David at the exhibit. We found out we both lived in Caracas, and he invited me out. The rest is history. We have been married for twenty-one years on April 13, 2012.

For two years I continued with the bank and we continued dating. After two years of dating, he invited me to Houston to meet his father and his brother. Unfortunately, his mother had passed away, so I never had the chance to meet her, which I much regret because I heard lovely things about her. I met his family and went back to Venezuela, and he asked me to marry him.

His birthday is July 13, we met on June 13, and we wanted to get married on a 13th. He said, "We'll look for the closest Saturday 13th of the year." That was January and the closest 13th on a Saturday was in April. We got married and lived in Venezuela for about two years and a half. I had a daughter a year later, and because of her, I resigned from the bank. My daughter's name is Stefani and she is now nineteen years old. From Venezuela we moved to Trinidad and Tobago when she was eighteen months old. She attended school in Trinidad.

The family unit in Latin America tends to remain closer and remain a family unit much, much longer than we do in the U.S. Here the family unit tends to break up after high school and during the college years. Young people start to find their own places. In Venezuela, even after the university, men who are in the ages of thirty to forty, as long as they are single, live with their parents. Even if they get married, they're still close. We get married and we are still tight and strong. I mean, we never leave the family.

As I said before, David wanted to move back to Texas. Our dream was this, getting a ranch and building our hacienda. I really like Texas because it is so big and most of the people have big hearts like that. The people of Texas are pretty open. I always compare them with the people in my hometown. I think one of the reasons I fell in love with Texas was George Strait!

As far as hobbies are concerned, I used to swim a lot when I was a teenager. Now, I ride my bicycle, in the street, in the road. I don't like gyms. I feel kind of claustrophobic in them.

I enjoy doing volunteer work in the community. I do voluntary work for the Raphael Free Clinic in Kerrville. I am translator there. I answer the phones, help with filing, a little bit of everything, as much as I can do there. Sister Marge and Sister Mary Ann who manage the clinic are very lovely and devoted ladies. They have many wonderful and dedicated volunteers, and it is an enjoyable place to volunteer for a very good cause. We are in this process of building the house, and the time seems to fly, but I'm planning on doing more volunteer work.

What's my legacy to my daughter, Carlos, and the young people of today? I always told Stefani that God gave her life, and my gift to her was Spanish. She speaks perfect Spanish. She came in first place in the District of Texas in Spanish, and she's going to be competing for the State of Texas in Spanish. She speaks fluent English, too. She attended Our Lady of the Hills High School in Kerrville.

It is very important to learn another language and also never to be afraid of trying anything. Go forward and reach high for any goals and opportunities that you may have. Life is not only for partying and entertainment. It is more than that. Today's youth may need to learn they can do anything in life, but to never to forget their goals. One final comment: I love Texas!

Ann Lyneah Curtis

Harper. Texas–Webster. New York

I'm from Webster, New York, which is right outside of Rochester in the upstate area. I lived there for eighteen years. Elder Brewster, who came over on the Mayflower, was one of my ancestors and so was Samuel Adams, the politician.

Life for me as a youngster and the conditions at that time were very strange and unusual. I was already into making art and I was a bit of a geek, but not in the way geek is nowadays with computer geek—I was just sort of a geek. I had a group of friends, but I was so different from the other kids that sometimes they didn't want to hang out with me. So I had a big fantasy world for myself.

I started telling the other kids that I was Martian and I was from Mars. I started using that a lot when I was creating my play characters and, of course, they teased me a lot. There were sad moments because some of the girls found that being my friend compromised their relationships with boys. I'm jumping ahead now, but I at the age of twelve all my neighborhood friends came to me and told me that the boys found me too weird and they wanted to be with boys at that point. They were ditching me and they were going to take my other friends away from me. Although they tried and there were a lot of sad times from twelve to fourteen, I had a fabulous home life. My home was stable and sound and my mother had a fabulous yard full of flowers. The back end of the last quarter-acre was all wooded and I built forts in there.

I lived in a neighborhood on two very short streets off of a main road and there was a lot of wooded area all around it. My brother and sister, who are older than me, had already built forts all around the whole neighborhood. This extended for miles, actually, and they made maps of the forts so I knew where they were. I took my dog with me so I would be safe because a lot of the neighborhood kids liked to put me in patches of poison ivy or torture me slightly because I was a geek, I was very different.

The fantasy world was highly encouraged in my family and I was encouraged to play dress up, yet I knew what was reality. I played dress up and I played with dolls until I was fourteen. I still play dress up. Dress up is fun. My mother played dress up. Creativity was encouraged, and I think that was why I said I was a Martian. I always had a place where I could go, in my room, in my head, and in my yard.

My parents were very much into the arts. My dad was a big band musician and at night he played saxophone and trombone. He also arranged music on the piano. He played clarinet and a little bit of guitar. I took lots of music lessons throughout my childhood and as soon as the lesson was over, I'd go draw.

My mother, who was born in 1918, wanted to be an actress. My dad was born in 1916. My mom was forty when she had me. She was a very talented artist, which I did not know until I was sixteen. That wasn't brought out because my dad wanted to raise us children as musicians. My sister was a premier singer and she was fabulous with an operatic voice, a lovely soprano. My brother, not so much. He ended up being a journalist major and who knows what he ended up doing. I was encouraged to be an artist, but I didn't know how much of an artist my mother was until a lot later. She was a fabulously creative person and wanted to be an actress, but actresses were considered whores when she was growing up.

As a teenager, about fourteen, I was in junior high and still dealing with being very different from everybody. My mom kept saying, "Ignore them, ignore them, ignore them." Ignoring people who are teasing you is hard because you want to throw things at them. But finally I began ignoring them and I developed a huge group of friends that were very diverse, from the freaks to the drama students. I was in drama and I was also on student council.

Ambassadors of the

At the age of sixteen, I started taking life-drawing classes with nude models at the Unitarian Church in Rochester. My mother would drive my girlfriend and me there, or her mother would, and drop us off and pick us up again later. It was a two-hour class and during that time they asked me if I would model. I said I'd have to ask my mother. You were paid $5 an hour, which was fabulous money back in 1972. She said if I wanted to do it I could. So I started modeling, and I was very nervous at that time because I was naked in front of a lot of people. It taught me a different way of looking at and working with the human body, which I'd been doing since I was about the age of ten.

When I was younger, I was drawing for my mother using a Frederick's of Hollywood catalog. Do you remember what they looked like back then? Daisy May sort of characters with bullet breasts. I would draw my images of women from that and I'd make them naked. I don't know why, I just did, and so drawing from life gave me a whole different perspective on how to draw. I learned more than I can tell you by taking those classes. Then modeling taught me how to work with form, but it also taught me a sense of self that was amazing and gave me a way to make a living right up until the age of thirty.

I was teaching art classes at a Montessori school for kids and they wanted me to teach full time. I quit all that to go off and join the Renaissance Fair. I began doing life casting. I did portraits for seven years on and off. I did it when business was good and I waitressed when it wasn't, or I would get a job. I did odds and ends and I modeled for art classes and I did portraits.

During my last year at San Antonio College I learned how to cast faces using plaster and putting straws up the nose. It was a forty-minute process that was a little difficult to deal with, as you can imagine. You have to lie down—a mustache would be a problem because it could rip out. Later I learned how to cast faces using a medical-grade plastic bandage. Most people, unless they're really claustrophobic, I can do that. I started having gallery shows, with my drawings, my nudes, my paintings, and life castings that I'd done of people. The life castings sold first, right off the bat. And then I'd sell the paintings. So the masks seemed to be a really great way to go. I started offering to make castings of people when I was living in San Antonio and people were really digging it.

Life casting, for me, is the ultimate portrait. It's the oldest form of portraiture on the planet. It dates back to 5000 B.C. and it's something all the great rulers had done as a way of carrying themselves into the future. When you dig up their graves you find a lot of death masks and life castings and those were the perfect portraits they could pass on to future generations. For me, it's fabulous because I'm able to give that to people and they're going to pass this on to the future.

I was doing Renaissance Fairs and I met Derek in Waxahachie at the Scarborough Fair. We ended up getting together over the course of the year. We talked about what we'd like to do and where we'd like to live and we began looking all over the country. We were doing Renaissance Fairs in Michigan, Colorado, New York, and of course, Scarborough. We kept coming back to Texas—Derek was familiar with Texas—and we looked at a few other places.

Derek's mom was dabbling in real estate at the time and she began to tell us about places around the San Antonio/Austin area. At about the same time my father died and my mother had died three years before him. I inherited $60,000 so we had that to play with. Derek's mother found this place in Harper that she thought we should look at, but it was an hour and a half away from San Antonio. We, of course, fell in love with the creek and the bluffs. But what really impressed us were the springs that feed into Ghost Hollows. Ghost Hollows is a box canyon on the property. It was beautiful and there was water in the creek and as we know there are a lot of dry creeks here in Texas.

The cost of properties was plummeting. We came out here and spent an entire day walking around and then we contacted the realtor. One of the things my parents instilled in me was: If you can't buy it, don't. We needed $10,000 to build a structure that we could live in and have enough money to buy the property, which is what we wanted. That's how we ended up in Harper, because this was a beautiful piece of property. There were no neighbors and we lived way out in the country, and with what we do for a living, we could live this far away from town.

What do I do for fun? Art! I like to sew and I like to walk around my property. I love to photograph and I do a lot of things with photographs, but everything I do feeds right back into making art. I document every year when I go traveling. We'll take off and go for a month here and a month there or for a few weeks. I document my year as it goes on as well as the people that I'm involved with and their costumes.

My legacy to the younger generation? Wow! It's a tough one because I'd like to tell them that they should do something they love. Again, our economy and the state of world affairs may be such that it is harder to do that now than it has ever been before. Have confidence in yourself, love yourself, and give yourself the opportunity to love what you do. Even if you're not doing exactly what you wish you could be doing. Hey, I wish I was independently wealthy and I could travel around the world and take art workshops where ever I go because they're so much fun. But I can't do that. Do I love what I do? Yes. Have I chosen to be independently employed? Yes. Is it easy? No. There are times when it's very much *not* easy. But it's important to love what you do. And if at any time you start questioning it, if it's too much, find something you do love to do. Find a way to make that happen. That's what I'd like to tell them.

Randy Schoenfelder, Policeman

Harper, Texas–Mitchell, South Dakota

I have seen so many people whose lives were ruined by drugs and crime. Be an honest and decent human being.

Jacques Vaucher

Harper, Texas–Lyon, France

I was born in Lyon, France, which is near the center of France, and I have been in Harper almost five years. Before I came to Texas, I was doing a show in Scottsdale, Arizona and I had a show to do in Daytona Beach, Florida. I was driving down with all my equipment to display and I had a week to kill. I called my wife in New York and I asked her if she would find me a ranch where I could ride horses. I really like riding horses and she found a ranch in Uvalde. I

Ambassadors of the

spent four or five days in Uvalde and I really enjoyed the area. When I went back to New York I told my wife this was a great place. I really enjoyed this part of the United States and we should look into it, because we were talking about moving out of the New York area.

I brought my wife back to Uvalde to see the ranch and she really liked the area, but she wasn't sure about the town. Some clients from her restaurant business in New York told her about Fredericksburg and she really liked it, so I stopped at the first real estate agent and we went to look at a few places around Fredericksburg and the area. We really liked Harper, even though it was a bit far away. We kind of liked the idea of living in the country, in a real country, a good country. And we are very happy here.

I had a very nice family during my early years. I have two great parents and they had four children—I was the second one. At first we lived most of the time in the country and that's probably why I came back to the country after living in big cities. We lived in Brittany and I remember that part of my youth best because I really enjoyed living in Brittany with a great family and a great village where people were nice. It was right after the war and Europe was building back up. I had a very good place in life and my parents were well-to-do. We didn't have any problems living there.

That little village in Brittany didn't have a school. My father built the school because he ran the factory and everybody in the village worked for the factory. Since there was no school and he had children, he built a school. I was a little bit spoiled because none of the children wanted to say anything bad to me, for obvious reasons. I had a sister who was the perfect student, and I was the "troubled" one. I was never great in school.

I had no responsibilities at home at that time—at that age I just wanted to be a kid. I went to school, played while I was in the school, but I didn't have to do anything important except be a kid. My parents always had horses, I had horses, and I always liked to ride.

When I was a teenager, my parents moved around a bit in France, and by the time I was a teenager I was living around Paris. Now, my after-school activities were when I had a good life. My parents had a hard time finding good schools for me. They knew I liked horseback riding, and one of the schools I went to had horseback riding every day. We had only one class in the morning and we went horseback riding in the afternoon. Another time we had skiing every afternoon and then a class in the morning. My parents knew I wasn't very academic.

After high school I went to the university, but I didn't finish it. I studied engineering because my parents were both engineers. I wanted to race cars but my father didn't think it was a profession, and it wasn't very much of a profession at that time. And since my parents didn't have any idea what I wanted to be, they sent me to engineering school. But in the 1960s there was a student revolution in France so my education was cut short and I didn't go back.

My mother was basically a mother—she wasn't working as an engineer because she had four kids and she had to take care of them. I'm the second child, and the only one that moved to the United States. My father traveled around the world doing his engineering business. He was hired by corporations to build up industries around the world. My sister, who was a pharmacist, just retired and she had a pharmacy in France. My other sister is a mother and she works for a book publisher. She publishes books for schools and sends them around the world. She's kind of winding down now, too. My brother is a computer fanatic. He's a troubleshooter with computers and he sees things in the future that involve computers. He works for a large university in France and they develop new systems.

I was always fascinated with cars—I liked speed and I liked racing cars. I went to racing school when I was in France. I went to England a lot because it was personal racing in Europe and I tried to get more involved with racing. I ended up being involved in racing in France, and I did some hill climbing and valleys. In Europe, I got involved in IMSA (International Motor Sport Association) and touring car championships. I went to work for Maserati, which is an Italian racing car company. I met a wonderful person who was a racecar driver, so I worked with him and he helped me with my racing.

I was into sales and I sold Maserati cars. After that I went to work for Ferrari where I met a few artists who used the automobile as a subject in their artwork. When I was working with Ferrari I started organizing some shows in the Ferrari dealership about artwork related to automobiles.

I traveled and I told my father I would like to go to the United States. I first came to New York City and I stayed there for the last twenty-five years. That's where I started my business and had a few jobs before that. I lived outside of New York City, in the country in upstate New York. I sell all kinds of media regarding the story of cars and racing cars, and also a few things about airplanes, boats, and motorcycles.

When I was in New York I had a gallery. Here, in Texas, we do much of my business on the Internet and websites. We organize auctions, mail-order auctions, and online auctions. We go to shows around the country, different events, racetracks, or vintage car auctions. In Europe, we actually have car clubs that come to visit. My wife was in the restaurant business and she can put on some great meals. We have a luncheon here for people who are touring the country with their cars or their motorcycles. We organize a lot of things like that—we have one next week with forty-three cars, I think. They are mainly British cars, like Jaguars.

Many of the people who come stay at the Inn of the Hills in Kerrville or in Fredericksburg. Texas has such great roads and that's one of the reasons I moved here. There's not much traffic and the roads are in good shape and they're all up and down and nice. I enjoy driving here—it's one of the reasons I like this area.

I have been married since 1996. We got married in Africa by a Masai tribe leader. We were the first and only white people the Masai tribe married. I was married before, briefly, when I was very young and it was a mistake, so we ended it and parted ways. I didn't want a traditional wedding, but Karen insisted on getting married. I was perfectly fine just living with her, but she wanted to get married so I said I'd get married if we could have a folkloric wedding. I was thinking maybe in Brazil, more like a feast.

Then Karen went to Africa to climb Mt. Kilimanjaro with a group of her friends. I went to meet her when she completed her climb because we were going on a camera safari together. I used to climb mountains when I was a kid. We went on a safari and during this safari, a guide said he would find a Masai tribe leader to marry us. He said this would be a wedding we would always remember.

It certainly was a different kind of wedding. The whole village was there, and as a matter of fact, the village next door was there, too. They were all dressed up in their native and festive outfits. They made me dress up as a senior warrior. They took us in their huts, where they made us up with makeup. It was great when the chief of the village, along with the medicine man, married us. We had a few friends as witness.

We didn't have any family members there for the wedding because when we left for Africa we didn't know we were going to be able to pull it off, so we didn't want to invite any family. In fact, my family couldn't believe it was for real, until I sent them a picture telling them we got married on such and such date. They said, "Oh, that must be one of Jacques' specials." Hey, it's a good way to remember your wedding.

I haven't gone back to Africa since the wedding. But I guess I'd be welcome as a senior warrior! Unless they don't remember me because that was a few years ago.

I always wanted to do what I liked to do and I worked very hard at doing it. I didn't say I like this and would like to do it. I went and did it. If you want something in life, you have to go and get it. You have to work hard at it and it's not easy, but at least you do what you please. What I would like to leave from my legacy is an awareness, because I had the first gallery that ever opened with this kind of artwork. To me it was important to make people aware these items existed. Before, it was just a few collector items and a lot of them were worn out. Now it's more of a lifestyle. I also hope I brought an awareness of enjoying the world. The younger people may not be driving cars much longer—they'll probably be driving computers. At least it'll be historical because what I sell is the story of the automobile from day one until the end, which may not be far away.

INGRAM

Ambassadors of the

Jose Santana, Restaurant Owner

Ingram. Texas–San Miguel de Allende. Mexico

A good education is something nobody can take away from you.

KERRVILLE

Bob Brunk

Kerrville, Texas–Grand Junction, Colorado

I have lived in Kerrville, Texas for the last thirty-two years, but I was born in Grand Junction, Colorado. My family lived in a town called Fruita, Colorado at that time. My dad worked for the county road department and my grandfather was the town commissioner. When I was not quite six, my family moved to a little town called DeBeque, Colorado, which was up the Colorado River about thirty-five miles from Grand Junction.

It was 1929, and the Depression was just starting to really hit. My dad had a good job throughout all that so I was really not affected financially. I was never hungry. However, the town was really small and almost everybody who lived in the community was on relief some way or another. Maybe half a dozen families were not. My mother was a bigoted woman, who was very bright, but she had a thing about people on relief. I was not allowed to associate with people on relief, which made my young life quite unhappy.

My mother was raised on a farm, and back in those days farmers had kids so they could work in the fields with them. My mother's family had three girls and only one boy, so the girls had to work in the fields, too. My mother was a hard-working woman who came out of high school and went to work in a big department store in town. Nobody had enough money to send her to school. My mom was a very bright woman and I think she was frustrated a good bit about her life. She was a good mother in terms of providing for us and keeping us clean.

My dad was raised in a Church of the Brethren family. He worked for a big commercial farming company called the Redland's Company. He drove a four-horse team pulling a big tank. He'd take that tank down to the river and fill it with water and haul it back for the stock.

My mother died in the fall of 1978. She was seventy-eight. Shortly after, I retired. My dad lived another ten years and was eighty-nine when he died. After my mom died, he married another woman not much older than I was. But he had ten great years with her and she really took good care of him.

When I was in the fifth grade, the school decided to form a school band. As a fifth grader, I was old enough to be in band. I had a sister who was fifteen months older than I am. She ended up being first chair clarinet and I was first chair cornet. As time went by, we all grew up and got into high school and we became a pretty darn good band with thirty members. I had good times at school.

The problem with the kids on relief persisted in my family. I was in trouble at home most of the time because those boys were good friends of mine and I had to do what I had to do. My dad just did whatever my mother said. If he came home from work and Mother said, "Your son needs a whippin'" I'd probably get a whippin'. This was a very rural area and we'd go out and shoot rabbits together. As we got older, we went hunting. But in school about the only real sport we had was basketball—I was always on the basketball team. We'd get together and play baseball in the spring. I continued my friendships after high school to the extent that I could. I left the little town of DeBeque in November of 1940 when I joined the Navy and I didn't live there again until 1946. By that time everybody was scattered out.

I didn't graduate from high school. I was a senior when I joined the Navy. One morning at the breakfast table, my father was upset at me, which resulted in a little scuffle. I suggested I should join the Navy, and that very day I did. I was

Ambassadors of the

in for five and a half years. When I came home I immediately took the GED and the old superintendent insisted on listing me in the graduating class of 1947. So I have a regular high school diploma. I would've graduated in 1941, but there were unusual circumstances.

I went to hospital corpsman school and I became a corpsman, and later a pharmacist mate. I was in Pearl Harbor on December 7. I had just gotten aboard in September on the *USS Curtiss*, a big seaplane tender named after Ben Curtiss, the aviation pioneer. I had relatives in Honolulu—two of Dad's cousins lived there. One couple were both schoolteachers in peacetime and even after the war, so whenever I could get liberty I was almost always with them. On the morning of December 7, I was having breakfast with one of the cousins and back in those days the radios were almost always on. The announcement came on the radio that the island was under attack. Military personnel, policemen, and firemen were to report to their stations.

Immediately, I ran out into the street. A young officer was going by in his car and he picked me up and dropped me off on the fleet landing. Boats were coming in from all the ships and loading up and dropping men off on their ships. Right in the middle of Pearl Harbor is Ford Island, which at that time was an airport station. I had to get to my ship, which was over on the other side of Ford Island. At that time, the *USS Nevada* had been trying to get under way. We were right behind the *Nevada* and it eventually beached itself. The destroyer *Shaw* was in dry dock and as we went by it took a hit and the bow was blown off it.

By the time we got to my ship it was listing so badly that the gangway was way above water. I climbed up the boat boom to get back on the ship and went to work. The ship had been hit twice and it had taken a 500-pound bomb down through one of the 5-inch guns plus an airplane had crashed on us. The ship got credit for sinking a midget sub, one of the little two-man subs, and I think four airplanes and two assists on the airplanes.

We were in our battle stations until late on December 8, because I think they were expecting to keep coming. In the evening of December 7, one of those little two-man submarines was discovered under the hospital ship source. They told us to get underway and, of course, the sub would get underway. Finally they got it tugged and towed the sub off—they really took care of that sub. I don't have any resentment towards the Japanese anymore.

I am an active member of the Pearl Harbor Survivors Association and I became aware of the organization in 1970. Every five years survivors return to Hawaii on December 7. My first trip back was in 1971. I went back for the fiftieth anniversary and our sixty-fifth anniversary; on the sixty-fifth I took my sons and their wives with me. In previous years, no survivors came to the reunion. Last year in Minneapolis, there was only one. One other survivor besides me.

I had a very rewarding career in the Navy. I think this was true of my working career, too. I was a medic. I started out as a hospital corpsman and I managed to make chief pharmacist mate before I came out. They call them hospital men now. I felt very fortunate and very blessed.

I came home on leave in 1943, and I remembered a girl from a little town thirteen miles away. I went up and knocked on her door. It was a Monday and I asked her if she wanted to go to a movie with me and she did. I saw her several times that week and we went out dancing with my folks that Saturday night. My leave was nearly up and I had to head home or head back to the ship the next Saturday night. I proposed to her and she accepted. It was quite a chore to get everything we needed done. We got our blood tests back from Denver and we had to send the rings to Denver to get sized and sent back.

Following my Navy career I went to work for the Colorado State Highway Department where my dad worked. He had a job waiting for me. It took about fifteen months for me to realize that the job wasn't for me. He thought I had lost my mind when I quit.

I moved to Grand Junction because they were building a V.A. hospital there. During this time I had the opportunity to use my G.I. Bill to learn to fly. While at the V.A. hospital, the office manager quit and they were looking for an office manager. I had the skills, so I went to work for them as an office manager and that lasted a little over two years. By that time, the V.A. hospital had opened and I had taken a clerk typist test. I was hired in the summer of 1949 as a clerk typist.

Opportunity came eighteen months later when I got promoted and moved to the personnel office of human resources. I was there a couple years and we had an audit and one of the auditors from Washington D.C. came down. For some reason he took a liking to me. After he got back to Washington, I started getting offers to transfer and got promoted. I was in Walla Walla, Washington where I retired as a hospital director. I had served in thirteen hospitals prior to that.

The V.A. had something to do with me coming to Texas. They transferred me to Houston in 1963, and in 1963 I turned forty. I thought it was time to start thinking about what I was going to do for the rest of my life. We started looking around to buy some retirement property. We heard about a big ranch—the old Stone Lee Ranch in Center Point—that was being broken up and sold in ten-acre parcels. We came up to Center Point and ended up buying ten acres of land. So we committed ourselves in 1963 to this area.

Some of the happiest moments of my life include being appointed hospital director and seeing my first grandchild. It was exciting. I have two sons. One son has three boys and the other son has one girl. I'd like them to know that I worked hard and that I was honest and that I loved my family and especially my wife.

Alberto Colin

Kerrville, Texas–Tlapujahua, Michoacan, Mexico

My full name is Jose Alberto Guadalupe Colin Marin. Why do I have five names? Most Latin people have more than one name and we have two last names. One is our mother's and one is our father's. I would like to explain the meaning of my three first names. When I was baptized, the priest made the decision to call me Jose Alberto, but before that my parents wanted me to be Alberto Guadalupe. When I was a little baby I got sick, very sick. My older sister promised Our

Lady if I recovered my health, she wanted to call me Guadalupe. After that they went to the priest to baptize me, he accepted it and they called me Alberto Guadalupe. So I have three names, Jose Alberto Guadalupe. The first two from my baptism and the other one corresponds to my birth certificate. Colin belongs to my father's side and Marin is my mother's last name.

I was born in Michuacan, Mexico in a small town called La Tlapujahua. My early years were normal for a young boy. I am the youngest of ten and I was very protected by my brothers and sisters and also my parents. Life for me was easy and I was a happy boy, and yes, sometimes I think I was very spoiled, very, very spoiled. That is why sometimes I think I was a rebel, but life for me was very easy and I was happy.

At my parents' home each of us had a special role or responsibility. My responsibility was to take care of the sheep. Yes, I was a shepherd at an early age and now I am a shepherd of people. I had to take care of all the sheep, going after them in the mountains and around the rivers. My father has very good grazing land and we were able to raise sheep, cows, chickens—it was like a farm. We had about seventy-five sheep and over a hundred cattle. During the day I went to school, but most of the time I took care of the sheep after 3:00 until it become dark. The days when I didn't go to school, I used to take care of the sheep from 8:00 A.M. to 5:00 P.M.

Did the sheep behave? No, no, no, no, no. I had a hard time with those sheep and they were not obedient to me. I loved them, but at times they ate the plants on the neighbor's land. My father had to pay our neighbor because of that and on several occasions he got mad at me. I told him that I did my best. But sometimes I wasn't doing my best because I was spending time playing with my neighbors or sleeping.

When I woke up, I didn't know where the sheep were. One time, the neighbor kept three of the sheep because the sheep ate their corn plants and I didn't tell my father. After three weeks he asked me what happened to those three sheep? And I just said, "I don't know."

After ten years I told him the truth. But I never told him what happened because I felt guilty most of the time. I was afraid because he had warned me, "If you do this again I'm going to do something to you." I was afraid because he didn't tell me what would happen to me and the neighbor never told him—he was happy because he had three of our sheep.

I left my parents' house when I was eleven, because in the town where my father had his farm we only had an elementary school and a middle school. The middle school was the kind of school where you study through the television. My father was not happy with that kind of education. He decided to give us the opportunity to study elementary school, but I told him I wanted to study somewhere else. So I went to live with my older sister.

Because I was not with my parents, my life as a teenager was different. I was more of a rebel because I didn't want to be obedient to my sister. I wanted to do whatever I wanted. I had a lot of problems with her. Also, I didn't have a lot

Ambassadors of the

of friends. I only had three friends, and only two were close friends while I was between twelve and fourteen years old.

At that time I made a decision to enter the seminary. Seeing myself being a rebel teenager, I realized my life was not going too well in my present environment before God's eyes. I was thinking more about the priesthood. I was fourteen at that time.

The first time I felt the call to become a priest was when I was eight. The first time I saw a priest celebrating Mass, I really enjoyed his reverence when he opened his arms in the moment of consecration. I enjoyed that part, and I said *I want to do that.*

After middle school I entered a high school that belongs to a religious community. It was like a Catholic high school. I tried to get more information about faith, tried to have an opportunity to meet more nuns, more priests, including seminarians. But I was a very quiet person and not open-minded, and I was very serious. I was not able to speak more than ten minutes to other people.

No one knew what I wanted to do. When I was in the eleventh grade, I was visiting my parents and I told them I would like to be a priest. They laughed at me because they knew I was a rebel. They laughed and said, "You're kidding us, it's not true."

Before I mentioned my goal in life, my father was not very religious and he didn't practice his faith. He told us that faith was only for women and not for men. So I was afraid to tell him that I would like to be a priest, but by the time I did tell him he had participated in a retreat and he had this conversion and he was very different. He began to see that I was serious and he asked me how he could help me to accomplish this.

School was wonderful. I could say I was a very good student because I loved to study. It was always a challenge for me to keep my record at school, and it is why I also became very quiet. I never spent too much time playing or with my friends and I was very persistent in my studies.

In middle school as I had told you I had only three friends, very close. But in high school I had more, which included a group of ten. There were four girls and six boys and we shared everything. It was a great opportunity for me to learn the real meaning of friendship because all of us helped each other in every way.

After high school I decided to enter a seminary. Even though I was studying in a Catholic high school, I didn't feel like a seminarian. The seminary was a religious community called The Society of St. Paul, whose purpose was to proclaim the good news of the gospel through the mass media. So after that, as seminarians, we had to get our degrees in mass communications besides the normal studies to become priests. In my case, I had to get my degree in philosophy and also mass communications, and that happened in that seminary.

I became a priest on January 19, 2009. My parents were so happy when I was ordained a priest, and they have told me many times that they are very proud of me. Besides being proud of me, they are worried about me. Even before I became a priest, they always told me, "If you want to be a priest, be a good priest because we don't need another bad priest. Be a good witness of God and try your best to bring people closer to God." That was their advice for me, and even now they always ask, "How is your community, how are you treating them, are you being patient with them?"

My mom is a very special person in my life. She is a very religious person. She said that one day when she was a teen she was attending a Mass and asked God, "If you give me children I will allow you to pick one of my children to be a priest."

She married my father and now we are ten in my family, eight men and two women. My mother always taught us how to be closer to God. Even my father was not ready to accept that, but she was teaching us underground. She was teaching us how to pray the rosary, how to make better sacrifices for God, and all of that.

The majority of my brothers and sisters were very happy about me becoming a priest. Only two of them thought I was lying and that I was taking advantage of the seminary to study something else. When I entered the seminary and after five years they realized that I was doing what I wanted to do and I was honest in my decision. When I became a priest, they felt like my parents, they were very happy with me and they felt special because finally God has chosen one of us to become a priest. My mother was happy because one of her children answered her prayers.

When I was in Mexico City I met Archbishop Jose Gomez, who was the auxiliary bishop in Denver. At that time I was in the seminary. I told him I wanted to be a missionary priest and he invited me to come to the U.S., to Denver. He said that diocese needed a lot of Hispanic priests, so I came to Denver and really liked it. I felt comfortable being a priest in the United States. But the archbishop was moving to San Antonio and he invited me to come to San Antonio. After two years of thinking about it I made the decision to move to San Antonio, Texas rather than stay in Denver.

After I became a deacon, my first assignment was to help Father Michael Pienemen here in Kerrville. After that I became a priest and he made me a parochial vicar in this parish for a period of three years. I have already been here two years and this is my last one.

When I ask my parishioners, "How are you?" I'd like them to answer me, "I am blessed." I feel God has given us everything. I'm a blessing for them and they're a blessing to me.

What legacy would I like to leave for my nephews, nieces, as well as the young people of today in the United States and Mexico? First of all, I would invite them to study more than the normal things, more than just to accomplish only the basic requirements. I would like them to study and be prepared for many things. When you are well-prepared you can face problems more easily. The other thing is do everything with happiness, enjoy life, and laugh even at your own mistakes. It's the only way you are going to improve yourself—if you pay attention only to your mistakes and never laugh at them you will become a very sad person, an angry person, and depressed. You will see your problems as big problems when they are really small problems.

I would like them to know that I'm a very normal person with a special mission in the world. I'm not an angel and I came like you from a real world with a normal life, but with big dreams. I want to be a holy person who is helping others to be holy in this life.

Dotte Dunne

Kerrville, Texas–Detroit, Michigan

I came to Texas in a roundabout way and it is difficult to know where to begin. I retired in Detroit, Michigan with my husband. We hit the road with our Airstream trailer, and we wanted to do a lot of traveling in the States first, which we did. We went to Mexico, and we loved it in Mexico, in Guadalajara. We stayed there about three years until my husband became ill. We brought him back to Houston, Texas where he died, and I returned to Mexico.

When we first came to Texas, people told us they always stopped at Kerrville on their way down to the Valley. I couldn't even find Kerrville on the map. This made me very interested and curious to know where in heck was Kerrville and

Ambassadors of the

why was it so good. After my husband died, I met someone else, and we were coming back to Texas. Someone told us, "If you're going to Kerrville be sure to go to the Take It Easy RV Park because they have a beautiful indoor swimming pool." I'm an avid swimmer, so that was all I needed. The first time I stayed for maybe three or four days, and I liked it so much. I went to Mexico, but came back here the following year, and stayed a little longer. Eventually, the man I was dating and I decided we would buy a place and settle in Kerrville, Texas. We did, and I've been here ever since he died, over twenty years. I never considered going anyplace else. I think I am going out feet first.

When I was a youngster, although we were very happy, we certainly didn't have much money. When I was nine or ten, the Depression came about. Every summer while my dad was laid off from Ford Motors or wherever he was working, we went camping up north in Michigan. We did that every single summer, and I loved it. We all swam, my parents too, and we really were very happy. I had one brother. That was our family, and that was our outing every summer.

I played tennis and baseball, girls'. At that time, in school when you had recess or gym—in the right season anyway—it was always baseball. You didn't have to be a boy to play baseball.

At home I had the normal chores, washing dishes and maybe working in the yard a little. I'm left-handed, and my mother always said I undid everything she did.

Life as a teenager was good. Because my health wasn't very good in Detroit, I lived up in north Michigan with my aunt and uncle for year, and that was where I graduated from high school. The air was a lot cleaner there than in Detroit. I skied, and had a lot of fun up north. There was a lot more snow, and hills and lakes in the summer for swimming and tennis.

When I was in Michigan, a couple of times we played hooky in the afternoon because it's so nice there. But nothing serious. I really enjoyed school.

After finishing school, I worked as a secretary. I started right in working. I worked in what they called Teletype–Postal Telegraph, which was like Western Union. That was my first real job right out of high school. I worked there four or five years I guess. After that, my husband was very old-fashioned, and he had the idea that his wife should not work and we would have children immediately, but that sort of fell through. So eventually, I got back to working a little bit. I worked at a store as a saleslady. Then I got back into office work. Then I worked with the Board of Education, which made us both happy because I had the summer off and we could take our vacations. He didn't like me working full-time anyway.

I went on to become a secretary in Detroit for a middle school. I was there sixteen years. It was very nice and, surprisingly enough, it was in an area where it was all black. My principal was black, and sometimes the assistant was, but sometimes not. The teachers were about half black and half white. At first it seemed strange, but I got along very well with them. My principal reminded me of my dad, he was a prince of a guy. And the kids treated me fine. I don't remember having a problem with them.

My husband was ready to retire—he was much older than I was. We definitely didn't plan that I would work after he retired. So we both retired the same day. Then we sold our house, signed the final papers, and we bought a trailer.

I loved Guadalajara, Mexico. Being up high, the weather was so nice. All summer long, you got maybe a little rain shower that would just settle the dust; it was never too hot because it was high. We lived in a trailer park. There were a lot of Americans there—mostly Americans. Anytime, right outside the gate of the park, we could catch a bus to go downtown or anywhere we wanted. We associated with the Mexicans all the time, and they were nice people. We liked them.

Every Sunday, the Degollado Theater had a show, the Folklorico. It was fabulous.

I never had any problems with safety. My friend and I had a deal for New Year's Eve. We would leave early in the evening, go downtown, take in a show, and then go out to a real nice place for dinner, and have our midnight there. We would walk back to the trailer park, maybe two or three miles. But we never, ever had any troubles.

The first big trip I took after I came to Kerrville was after my husband died in 1983, because we always did everything together. A lady I played bridge with was looking for someone to go on a freighter trip with her. I didn't know her very well, but thought that sounded fantastic. On a freighter trip, you never know how long you're going to be gone. It ended up we were gone 120 days. Four months.

We left towards the end of June, and you never know for sure when you're going to get on the boat. We took off not knowing where we were going. We were in a little town in Italy that was just north of Spitz, Yugoslavia. We kind of hung around there for three or four days while they were repainting our ship and bringing it up to date.

We went as far as Australia and New Zealand. It was nice when we were in Australia, we got to go to an opera. We saw Perth, Australia. We had a beautiful pool that we got to use all the time, except when we were docked. They wouldn't change the water then because the water's not clear when you're in dock. We spent about four days in Saudi Arabia. The trouble there was we could not get off the ship. The Saudis wouldn't even let us stand on the dock. They were loading the ship and one of the sailors had a brother on another ship that was docked there, and they wouldn't even let them get together to talk. We could see those beautiful cities, but they wouldn't let us put a foot on the dock. I supposed it was because we were American. They are so particular. We always had wine on the table, but when we were there we couldn't even have wine or vinegar on the table. Coming back we were in France, in Marseille.

Later, I took a lot of tours with a girlfriend. We did Norway and all those countries. We went on a safari in Africa. We did China—I loved China, and Japan. I liked southern France—I guess it was the sunshine and the flowers. The weather was so nice. We got to go through perfume factories. I loved Ireland, too, no doubt about that. But I really liked southern France.

Ambassadors of the

I still swim everyday. I don't do as much actual swimming as I'd like to be doing, but we have water aerobics five times a week and then we play water volleyball three times a week. So every day I'm in the water.

I've been a member of the Trailblazers for eighteen years. It's a wonderful organization. I think you know the AVA is the American Volkssport Association. Volkssport means walking in German. We have 10K walks that we do every now and then, different Saturdays they have sanctioned walks, many of which are in San Antonio. At least four clubs are there and they put on walks. If you are going to belong to the organization, you must put on at least one walk a year. It has to be planned ahead, it's organized, you have a distance planned and checkpoints, and you get credit for those. Of course, we go for the credits.

The longest I've walked I suppose is twenty miles. I've taken a lot of walking trips, too. And we go to conventions where they have walks every day, so that's part of the fun of it. You get to do a 10K walk every day. We met an English lady who does walks in Scotland and Ireland. For several years I did walks with her all over Scotland and Ireland, which was fun.

I think the main thing is to be friendly and like people. Smile at people. Some people say when you get to be my age that the younger people don't like you. I don't have that problem. Most of the people I associate with are younger, and they don't seem to resent me. In the RV park, I'm with younger people all the time. The people I take trips with are all younger, and they don't seem to mind as long as I keep up. And I do. I think you've got to have a good attitude.

(Dotte has been a line dancer for many, many years. She still attends line-dancing classes on Monday, Wednesday, and Friday. She goes to a yoga class two days a week. She teaches an exercise class several days a week. She does a lot of gardening. She loves to read. She also has season tickets to the Kerrville Symphony as well as the KPAS programs. She says she tries to live a very Christian life and she is a young ninety-year-old.)

Gisela Hecklau

Kerrville, Texas–Schlettau, East Germany

I was born in East Germany, and when the Russians came, we went to West Germany. We then immigrated to the United States and landed in Milwaukee, Wisconsin in November of 1951. We lived there from 1951 to 1979. We arrived in Kerrville, Texas in 1979.

What attracted us to Texas was the weather. We had so much snow and ice in Wisconsin in the winter and that was not for me. I'm an outdoor girl and I

Ambassadors of the

want to have air. We came to Kerrville after looking at information about cities in Texas. My oldest daughter lived in Houston and during one of our trips to Mexico we stopped in San Antonio. I felt these cities were too big for us, and they were very hot and humid. I saw a small pamphlet about Kerrville and this is what I wanted rather than a big city, because I grew up in a small village next to a city. We drove around the hills of Kerrville to see the trees, river, and everything I saw I really liked that first day. After our two-week visit here we went home, sold our house, and moved to Kerrville. I have lived here for over thirty years and I really like this place.

I have three daughters, two in Kerrville and one in Chicago. However, my husband passed away in 1995. The daughter who formerly lived in Milwaukee has been living here for the past four or five years. The one who was in Houston also has come to live here. My daughter who works in Chicago will come here when she retires.

Life for me as a young child in Germany was wonderful. We had a big home and a big garden in our little village, which was only ten minutes from the city. We went to school in the city.

Life as a teenager was a wonderful time. School was very important and we all got together for sports. I was a good student, but I was a little lazy. I thought I didn't need this because I was a girl, but it was fun. Our first four years of education were in our village and sometimes there were three classes in the same room. At ten years old, we attended school in a nearby city named Halle.

From the age of ten we took English and then French and all the other subjects. At that age the boys and girls were separated into different schools. If we didn't pass the exam at age ten we had to go to craft schools where students learned a trade. It was required that students attend school until they were fourteen years old.

I did a lot of fun things after school. Rowing a boat for the regatta with four girls in the boat with professional oars was my favorite. I still have an oak leaf made of copper I got when we won a race. I also had singing and tap dancing lessons. I skied in the winter and went swimming in the summer.

When I was nineteen, going on twenty, I was introduced to a German officer and eventually we married. The war started soon after we were married, but we were not affected because we were in the middle of the country. My brothers were in the war and they fought against the Russians. Hitler told us we would gain our land back and he marched on.

People said Hitler corrupted the churches and that was a no-no. He himself was outcast from Austria and he didn't like the elite group he had around him with the black uniforms. We heard they were not allowed to go to church. But, we people got married in church and had our kids baptized, also.

My husband and I moved to another place, but he was never home. The only people left in our town were the old people and mothers with young children because all the men were in the war. Then came the bombs that fell all the time. It got worse and worse. They bombed everything, including the railroad station and the city. I had two children at the time, one six months old and the other three years old. We went to the basement, which was very strong, and we were somewhat safe. All around me everything was burning and the next morning there was nothing out there.

We were fortunate, but very dirty from all the dust because all the windows were blown out. I found a baby buggy and a stroller. Someone announced on a speaker where we should go. I must have walked for more than three hours with these two carriages to the French station, which was far out of the city. They put us in wagons to take us to the next city, which was Halle where I came from. People were very nice to us. They watched my children and gave them something to drink. I had to take another smaller train for ten minutes to get back to my parents in that little village because the bombs didn't fall there. My apartment was all damaged and I stayed with my parents.

Seven American officers stayed at our house and it was wonderful. One day they didn't come back. Then the Russians came in their wagons pulled by horses.

When my husband came back from the war he was given two choices by the Russians: He could work in a factory or become a Russian teacher. He chose to become a Russian teacher because he was intelligent enough to learn another language. He was taught how to teach and they paid him for it. He didn't like what he had to tell the schoolchildren, that is, Russia is so beautiful and supposedly had many beautiful things to see there. Also, that Germany was done and would be forgotten.

We decided we needed to get out of East Germany. My aunt lived in Wisconsin, and she invited us to come there and she would be our sponsor. We decided we had to get to West Germany. My husband had an uncle who farmed near the border and he was allowed to plant anything he wanted. The uncle explained to us that the border isn't a straight line but zigzags. He said, "Take a bicycle and put on apron and the guards will think you live here on our farm and they won't do anything."

I decided to walk near this guardhouse to see what was happening. Our friends thought I was nuts. I noticed how the guards walked around the guardhouse and then moved out in another direction, which was their route to guard. They continuously went up and around that area. The uncle drove us in a horse and buggy at 2:00 in the morning with my children to the border and I knew exactly where I wanted to go. I started walking toward the guardhouse, but I waited until I saw the guards walking away and when I couldn't see them anymore I stepped past the guardhouse. There were no mines or barbed wire fences yet so we went. If we were caught we would have been shot. They did kill one of my cousin's wives.

I sent my husband first across the border before I went. I told him to send me a telegram that he'd made it because he couldn't call write or call me. I got the telegram.

I walked over and we stood still and the children weren't harmed. The little one was only two and a half and this was no man's land. The field had been plowed and it was hard to walk because the land was uneven. I said to myself, *Dear God I try my best, but will you please help me a little?* When I looked up I

Ambassadors of the

couldn't believe what I saw. I saw two men walking toward me from the west and I wondered why they wanted to go back to the Russian zone because everybody wanted to get out.

They said they were looking for the path to the west but couldn't find it. I told them I knew how to get there but I needed their help. My little one couldn't walk anymore because she was exhausted. I told one man to take a bag and the other to take my youngest child. We walked and we walked for a long time. Finally, we came to West Germany and the English road there. I told the authorities these gentlemen needed a refugee camp and I knew where to go.

My brothers stayed in West Germany after the war. We immediately contacted the consulate in Frankfurt and started the paperwork. We found out we had to wait two years to immigrate to the U.S., but that was okay. I had a lot of family and friends there, but when we wanted to go they told us it would be about six months longer. I made friends with an American colonel and his family. He went with me to the consulate and we waited for two hours. He insisted they check for the papers and they finally found them. I don't know what I would have done if he wasn't with me.

A doctor checked us out and didn't find anything wrong with us, so we could go. The colonel took our stuff back with him when he returned home to Chicago. We met the colonel and his family in Chicago and he had two big crates for us. They stayed with us for several days and then went to San Francisco, California to live. We kept in contact with them for years. He did us a big favor and we never forgot it.

We then moved to Milwaukee, Wisconsin, and lived with my aunt and uncle for a while. I found work after one week in a factory. I worked next to a Jewish girl who was in a concentration camp. She told me some of her family members did not live through this because the soups were poisoned. She told me a man knew which barrel the poison soup was in and said not to drink from that barrel. They tried to help, but the German people didn't know what the commanders of the camp were doing to their captives. We found out when talking to other people that the average person in Germany, Poland, and Russia didn't know what their leaders were doing. We were treated very nicely by everyday people. Even my brothers were fed and were not harmed by the Russians.

My children do not remember what it was like when we had to cross the border. I think it was too much commotion for them. Although I like to forget all this, I only share my story if I like the people and know they will understand my experience. I have gone back to Germany to see relatives and friends, but it not the same anymore. The young people have no idea what life was like during the war and it is mostly tourists there now.

It is very important to maintain good health and have strong faith. You see, I very seldom prayed for a lot of things when I was at the border. It was the first time I seriously prayed to God to help get us safely across the border. Faith is very important to me. Another important thing is responsibility. Most young people want everything right now, but it is important to work hard for things you want and not expect people to give you everything. Also, think and plan thoroughly in whatever you do in life. In crossing the border I had to plan very carefully because it was a matter of life and death. My children and I were at the mercy of very cruel people. Thinking and planning are very important in whatever you do.

Norman Newell

Kerrville, Texas–Pardeeville, Wisconsin

I lived in Wisconsin most of my life, until twenty years ago. I came to Texas and settled in Kerrville because sometimes, when you're married, you do things your wife wants you to do. She had a friend she went to college with who had come to Kerrville. So, we stopped at Take It Easy RV Park—we'd been coming here for about twenty years before we settled in pretty much permanently.

My parents had absolutely nothing but us children. My dad worked on a farm and there were seven of us children. I was the second child and had a sister two years older than me. Dad made about $2 a day as a farmworker from the time he was married. So anything I needed or wanted, I went out and earned it from the time I was five years old. I would take an ax and go to neighbors' homes to see if they had any wood. If they did, I'd split that pile of wood for a nickel or a dime. I always asked my neighbors if they had any chores they could hire me to do. That was how I first made money. From then on, I was always looking for something to do. I picked strawberries for so much a quart or a pound. I picked cherries, too—sometimes I picked 800 quarts a day. I bought five different bicycles while I was growing up, and I always earned all the money to buy them.

The kids all called me "Happy Hooligan." There was a character in the funny papers named Happy Hooligan and guess I was as happy as he was, so that's why they called me that.

My teenage life was very busy. When I was seven or eight years old I hunted and trapped—that was one of the main activities of my youth. I trapped a lot of coons, mink, weasels, and muskrats. I'd set my traps, then crawl under a brush pile to sleep. There were always brush piles wherever you went those days, always full of leaves, and that's how I kept warm. I'd wake up the next morning, make my breakfast, and go out and look at my traps. One afternoon, I set out thirty traps and I had twenty-eight muskrats in the morning. Skinned them myself and cured them out. Probably a month later I'd sell the pelts to fur buyers. I'd take them home and stretch them out, tack them up outside, and they'd cure. The price would go up and down, and when the price was up I'd sell them. I only trapped for the fur so I could make some money. I trapped in the winter, too, set out traps before I went to school.

I went through five grades of school, and from then on it was all about making money. I don't think either of my parents went further than fifth grade. My dad allowed me to do pretty near anything I wanted to do because I never got into trouble.

Sometimes in the morning I also worked for an ice company that delivered ice to the houses in town. They'd probably put up about 10,000 tons of ice, and that would carry through the summer. I worked on the lake, helping put up ice. I always got there about 6:00 A.M., when it was generally zero degrees—it was 48 below zero one morning. They sawed the ice about a foot down with a buzz saw, then they would get a channel through the ice so they could float the ice to the loading dock. Then they pulled it up a chute and loaded it onto trucks. They hauled five, six, seven tons of ice on a truck to a place where they piled it, one block on top of the other, and they packed it in sawdust to keep it from melting in the summer. I made 25 cents an hour. It was pretty good money for that time. I was a teenager.

In the summertime, at that age, I shot gophers. In Wisconsin, they paid a bounty on gophers because they ate farmers' crops. I was an expert shot. I took a .22 and put it across my bicycle, and rode up and down the roads all over Wisconsin. If I saw two gophers, I lined them up, knelt down so they were in perfect line, shot—and I'd have two gophers.

Ambassadors of the

I trapped all over. I read in a magazine that Mississippi and the southern states were where most of the muskrats were trapped. So I was real interested in going down there. I built a little boat on my own, and traveled down the Mississippi River. I was about nineteen at that time. I put it in the Wisconsin River to begin with, but it got cold and froze up, so then I shipped it down to the Mississippi. I went 1,155 miles on the Mississippi River. I shot birds and took the meat, the breasts and legs, and put it in with beans. That's how I lived all the way down the Mississippi.

When I got to New Orleans I found out you had to lease the area you trapped, then you had to split the hides with the landowners. Before I got to trapping, I decided I was better off going back to Wisconsin and doing my trapping there. I shipped the boat and the traps back. All freight trains then had ice compartments in them, so I got up into the ice compartment on a train that was going north, and that's how I traveled back to Wisconsin. It took about two weeks to get back, from train to train, always going north. Then I went back to chopping ice again.

I hunted gophers until I made enough to buy my first new car. I traveled out West and started building buildings for the Army and Navy. That was in Idaho, on Lake Coeur d'Alene. Then I got interested in going deep-sea fishing on the ocean. I bought a 30-foot boat, and the first trip out, I put two tons of ice on it. I caught 122 tuna my first day out. The next day, I don't know how many I got, but I had the boat pretty well loaded. I think I had about three tons of fish, maybe more than that.

I fished off of Oregon, Washington, and California. Then I got a 40-foot boat. I'd take on fifteen tons of ice and stay out two weeks—always two weeks. By myself. Took steaks that I iced down, each in a different ice compartment so I could get to them day by day. I'd ice down the fish, and then I'd always have a steak for the next day. I was out everyday, even if it was blowing 70, 80, 90 mph, I'd still be out there. Some of the time, I had to leave the lines out for a while 'til it cut down a bit. But I was always out.

When I came into the dock area with a big load of fish, the owner of the cannery asked how come I had so many fish. I said, "The weather is really bad out there." He offered me a job to buy fish for him up in Alaska. And he offered me a fabulous wage to take an 80-foot boat out to Prince William Sound and buy fish for him. So I accepted his offer, and the next spring, I took this 80-foot boat up to Prince William Sound, Alaska. I bought fish for him for about a month, then told him I planned to buy my own boat and go fishing.

I kept on fishing up there in Cordova, out of what they called the Mud Flats. I also took that small boat to Kodiak and fished there. I caught loads and loads of salmon there. From there I went back to Prince William Sound again and fished. I never did go back to the lower states to fish because the fishing was so much better up there. But I fished just salmon up there.

I sold fish to the same person the whole time I was there. I was thirty years old when I first started and I fished there for five years. I fished and hunted and trapped until I made enough money to buy anything I wanted.

I met my wife in 1952. That was the most exciting time of my life. I got married the last year I was there. My wife fished all summer with me, and that fall she said she'd had all the fishing she wanted. By that time, I had made enough money to buy a farm.

I bought a farm in Wisconsin—740 acres, with livestock and machinery. I bought the whole works. When I first started farming, I bought a lot more machinery and built a barn that was 220 feet long by 52 feet wide, with a basement under the whole thing so the manure just dropped through the floor. Then I just pumped it out and used a sprinkler a system to put it out onto the land. I farmed for the next twenty-five years and bought land that was for sale around me. I had 1,729 acres. When I was farming I had a little better than 800 cattle.

The government put loads and loads of farmers out of business. When I got through farming, when I finally retired, I decided to go around the country and let people know all about it. I put together three floats that I took around to different colleges and celebrations, where there were a lot of people. The float I enjoyed most was one that had a big davenport on the back with young ladies in swimming suits sitting on it. I had a bar in the middle of the float and a guy on the floor with a bottle in his hand—he was supposed to be drunk. Another fella was chasing a young lady around this bar and he was supposed to be drunk, and she was supposed to be one of his secretaries from Washington. On the side I had "Your tax dollars at work." I got the biggest ovation from the crowds with this float. The college kids were just nuts about that float. I put out a newspaper, and the head of it said "Congress: Untouchable Criminals."

When I retired from farming, I sold all my machinery and cattle. Then I went to northern Wisconsin and bought 9.5 acres on an island. It had a large house and a three-stall garage. But you couldn't drive to the island in the summertime because there was no bridge to the island. I put a 10-foot-wide path down along the water and back to the house again, and it was the best place on earth at that time. I lived there seventeen years before we retired to Texas.

I bought a diesel motor home and we traveled all over for ten years. We stayed here at Take It Easy RV Park for ten years before we finally bought a place to live here permanently. One of the reasons we chose this place is because it had a swimming pool, and we could go swimming every day. I was a pretty good swimmer. I got all kinds of Olympic medals in the Senior Games, and ten gold medals for winning in swimming at Take It Easy RV Resort. I was eighty years old.

We traveled all around the world, to Africa, India, China, New Zealand. These were places I always wanted to go to when I was a youngster. We went back to Wisconsin every summer and stayed there for a month to start with, then we got down to two weeks, then finally got down to probably ten days. We sold our motor home and now we're just staying at TIE. When we go back to Wisconsin now, it will be by car.

The education I've had, I wouldn't trade for anybody's education. The best part of my life has been work. Never, ever be afraid of work. Work is an exciting

Ambassadors of the

experience. And it can be the best thing that ever happens to anybody—to have a working background that you can be proud of. I have done everything.

I always ate right all my life. I eat lots of beans, and we ate lots of beans as a family because we had very little money. We always raised a couple of big sacks of beans. We thrashed them out ourselves with a pitchfork and canvas. We'd take the beans and hold them up and let the wind blow the chaff out. We always raised a big garden, and put up on average 400 quarts of vegetables. When I was out trapping, I always took a pail of beans and a paper sack. At night, I'd shoot some blue jays or robins and take the legs and breasts and put them in with the beans. I never ate fat because it's unhealthy for you.

We ate more venison than anything else. I always was in good health. I always had tough jobs and I was in good shape because of the work I did. My work was always outside all my life. I didn't have much school education, but I was schooling myself all the time. I never ran into problems that I couldn't figure out myself.

When I reached the young age of ninety-five I surprisingly received many birthday cards and telephone calls with best wishes from many of the people who'd worked for me over the years. It was then that I realized I was not only helpful, but I encouraged people who worked for me to work hard, to be dependable and responsible. They all ended up getting very good jobs in their careers. I guess I finally realized I went through this world and I didn't do too bad serving as a mentor to these young people.

Lloyd Painter

Kerrville, Texas–Dos Palos, California

I was born in a small town in central California called Dos Palos, population about 4,000. From there we moved to a smaller town of about 420. I went through all eight grades in a two-room school with a total of thirty students in the school. We had two teachers; one was also the principal.

My family was very poor. We lived in what I would consider today to be substandard housing. But we lived out in the country. I fished, I hunted, I did fun things that a young person should be able to do. And I grew up basically without supervision from my parents, because in those years, kids just grew up.

School was never a problem, I just studied and passed and went through it. I enjoyed school until the twelfth grade. I was valedictorian, by the way. I did not enjoy the five years at the university because I had to work very hard.

When I hit my teenage years, we moved to the town of Dos Palos, where I was born. My teenage years were filled with a tremendous amount of work. Farm labor—I actually picked cotton. I worked hard in the fields. My biggest goal in life at that time was to get away from that.

I think what motivated me was my parents didn't have any money. I knew that if I didn't go to school I was going to end up like them. The local community

Ambassadors of the

college offered free tuition, free books. I went there for two years, and then transferred to the state university. I worked my way through school the whole time. I worked in supermarkets. I really enjoyed it. Because I was a checker, I was making good money, and I had a healthcare plan. I was set. So I dropped out of college.

Just about the time I was twenty-one, I got my pre-induction physical for the Army. I was going to Vietnam. I had no deferment; I couldn't get out of that because I wasn't in college anymore. So I joined the Navy Reserve in Fresno. I went to California State University at Fresno. At that time it was Fresno State. The Navy Reserve allowed me to start attending meetings, go to boot camp as an enlisted person, and if I finished the university I could take the Officer Candidate School test. After I finished college, that's exactly what I did. I ran back to college and finished. I received a degree in criminal justice. It was a kick in the rear but I made it. I attended Officer Candidate School in Newport, Long Island, graduated in 1965 in March.

I finished college and went into the Navy, and they put me in the naval intelligence. I spent five years in naval intelligence traveling around the world. I married my beautiful wife, Ingrid, in Germany while I was stationed there and came back home.

I had been involved in a conflict in the Middle East, the Six-Day War, and I got wounded. I received a Purple Heart. When my five years were up and I had served my commitment, the option was to extend. They said I'd probably go to Southeast Asia and I said, "I've already been shot once, so just send me home to California."

I came home with my wife. I applied for many jobs and got one as a probation officer in Kern County, Bakersfield, California. In the meantime, I had gone to a post office in Fresno, California where I saw a huge picture of a fellow in the full uniform of President Nixon's Executive Protective Service, which today is the Uniform Division of the Secret Service. You could tear off a coupon at the bottom, fill it out, and send it to Washington. The salary was $7,000 a year. I told my wife, "At this point this is better than anything." So I sent it in.

Meanwhile, I became a probation officer and forgot all about it. Several months later I got a call from the Fresno office of the Secret Service. The caller said because of my education and background I qualified to be an agent. My life had been California; I knew the structure of the California law enforcement, but I had no vision of federal programs. He said, "Bring your wife in on a Saturday afternoon and I'll come in and we'll sit down and talk." Turns out he was one of the fellows in JFK's car when he got shot.

He talked to us for about an hour or two, and he said, "Well you've just passed your oral exam." That's how they did it then. Then he said, "Now you just have to take the test, but if you fail the test we'll bring you on board anyway for a year and we'll tutor you so you can pass it."

I told him I'd lost my top secret clearance when I married my German wife—they yanked my clearance. But I got my top secret clearance back. When they finally offered me the job I was working as a probation officer. I almost didn't take it because I enjoyed my probation job, but I did finally agree to it and twenty-eight years later I retired.

I was hired in 1970 in the Sacramento, California field office. From there I went to the Los Angeles field office and from there to the Gettysburg field office. I went to other field offices in the country, too, including Washington, DC, and retired from the San Francisco office.

I protected all the presidents from Nixon to Clinton. During those years, I was very nonpolitical. I became more political with age probably. In those years the presidents were people we protected. My favorite was Ronald Reagan because he was the kind of fellow you could sit down with, like he was one of us. Just a nice guy. I think everything you've read about him, or know about him, probably says that. The rest of them were just people we dealt with and it didn't make any difference to me.

I didn't consider it a job, it was an adventure most of the time. I was in it before 9/11. After 9/11 the Secret Service moved into Homeland Security. The few years I was in, and before, it was in the Treasury Department. We protected the president, the vice president, the former president, heads of state. We also investigated all threats made to those individuals, either written or e-mail. It's probably pretty similar today. We also investigated the financial part, the counterfeiting currency, bond forgery, check forgery, and in later years a lot of computer crime fraud. But when I worked, physical protection and intelligence threats kept us busy most of the time. Those took priority over everything.

I think most of my motivation early in life was negative—I did not want to be like my parents. I did not want to be poor. My father did a lot of things and nothing really well. He always seemed to start a business and it would fail. We were always poor and that's what I remember about my childhood. My mother is still poor to this day. I wanted to escape, and I realized I wasn't dumb. I had some innate intelligence, not a lot, but enough maybe to make it. And probably some street smarts, how to get things done and do the right thing. I learned growing up that certain things you have to do to get by.

My mother is ninety-five and still alive. My father passed away at seventy-two from lung cancer. He was a heavy smoker. My sister is sixty-five. That's my immediate family. My daughter is almost forty. She has a PhD in psychology and she's a doctor and a professor for two universities as an online professor. She teaches from her home. She lives in Woodbridge, Virginia and she's married to a soon-to-be lieutenant colonel in the Air Force.

One of my high school teachers inspired me in a negative way. I was told that I should take woodshop, and learn the trade and not to pursue anything. They did that then, back in the fifties. That angered me and motivated me more than anything. I had another teacher in my community college who really raked me over the coals in class because I wasn't up to speed on what he was teaching. I came from a rural high school and some of our teachers were farmers who came in part-time. I didn't have the background and I had a hard time staying up with it, but I did it.

Ambassadors of the

My journey to Texas is not hard to explain. My daughter—our only daughter—lived in San Antonio and is married to an Air Force officer. She had been bugging us for years to come to Texas. I told my daughter I didn't like most of Texas that I seen because it's hot and dry, and I don't like big cities. She found Comanche Trace Tour Homes in 2004 and asked us to come look. We came and looked and bought a lot and built our home. We no sooner got here than our daughter moved to Virginia. So we're in Texas, but we're loving it. The Texas Hill Country fit the bill for us.

One of the reasons we left California is because the medical profession there was so overwhelmed. I got sick a couple of times and I couldn't get into the hospital. I went to the emergency room on a weekend with kidney stones and I could not get in because of all the people coming in by ambulance, most of whom probably weren't citizens, quite frankly. I sat there four hours, passed the kidney stones, and went home. This happened two times on the weekends and finally the third time I got to see a doctor.

At that point I decided we had to leave, we could not get any older there. That was somewhere between 2002 and 2003. Plus, my daughter was living in San Antonio and the pull to Texas was becoming stronger and stronger. When we moved here in 2006, I had to go to the emergency room at Sid Peterson Hospital. I walked in at 7:30 in the morning and nobody was waiting there. I asked the nurse, "Where is everybody?" She said, "There were no accidents on I-10 last night." And I told my wife, "We've arrived."

Fortunately, or unfortunately, I got the horrible flu that went around a couple of years ago while I was in California and I came here with it. I ended up in the hospital in Kerrville for nine days, in intensive care. It was the best medical care I ever got in my life. I couldn't have been more happy to have been here with that problem. That was a big, big factor for me. This is great city in which to live because there's no crime to speak of and good medical help.

One thing I didn't have that my daughter will have is something of value that I leave behind, the house or whatever. I will leave them with something rather than what happened in my family. I want to leave them something rather than being a burden to them.

John Riedman

Kerrville, Texas–Valley City, North Dakota

I lived on a farm in North Dakota with 580 acres for twenty-one years and in South Dakota for twenty-three years. I grew up in the latter part of the Depression—I was born in '36, right at the tail end. Our house was very old and we were poor people, very poor. One of the greatest things we struggled with were dust storms. These horrendous storms made it literally black out during the day. When the storm was over, all the ledges of the house had a quarter-inch of dust on them, dust over everything, so a huge cleaning process followed. The state tried to combat the dust storm problem by developing what were called "Shelter Belts." The government provided trees for farmers to plant, strategically placed so the wind wouldn't get into their homes. We planted three major Shelter Belts. After the dust storms, all these new plantings would be covered up with dust. So the younger kids in the family dug out each tree as we went along.

Ambassadors of the

Eventually, that was the solution in North Dakota. Those Shelter Belts prevented the winds from developing significantly because they were planted throughout the state. It also increased the rainfall because we had more oxygen from the trees and that produces rain.

We went to grade school in one of those country schools. Everybody laughs when you talk about walking two and a half miles to school and the same back home. We literally did that. There were no rides. The only time I remember a ride was in a huge snowstorm. My dad hitched up the horses and took us to school on the sled and picked us up. This lasted for one or two days until we could walk it again.

As teenagers on the farm, we worked from the time we got up until time to go to school and then we worked when we got back home. The older ones were on the tractors and moved the manure from the cows and hand-milked the cows.

We went to school where the Sisters were. During school days we studied and, as typical kids, we horsed around a lot. In those days the punishment was staying after school and scrubbing something—scrubbing floors or chalkboards or taking out the trash. Did I scrub a lot of floors? Yes, I did. Oh, yeah.

I was probably an average student or lower "B" as far as marks. Math was terrible, I couldn't do math. English I enjoyed as well as history, geography, and biology. Physics was hard but I liked it because I was doing hands-on things. But math, I just couldn't see any sense to it. I would never use it anyway.

After high school I went directly to the Minor Seminary. The Minor Seminary was a college with courses in philosophy. Then I went to St. John's University in Collegeville, Minnesota where I majored in classical languages and in philosophy. I also minored in English and in education. I took eighteen hours at least every semester, the entire time I was in college. I was there four years for philosophy and then in Major Seminary taking theology for four years, so I was at St. John's a total of eight years.

All my brothers but one got married and had families, and so did my sisters. I have many nephews and nieces, thirteen, I think.

The decision to become a priest was a difficult one. In those days, you didn't want to disappoint your parents. They encouraged me and that was always on my mind. My mother was a Lutheran who had converted to Catholicism, but her side of the family was all Lutheran. Also, I enjoyed people and wanted to make people's lives better. I always saw the priesthood as the ultimate way to be invited into people's lives, and then I could bring them closer to God and the values that we need to make life worthwhile and relationships good.

I've probably done everything I'd wanted to do in life as a priest. I refereed basketball for twenty-seven years. I was a scoutmaster and have been involved in that program for years. Those were two things I enjoyed a lot. I did a lot of skiing. I love to play tennis so we played a lot of tennis. The meditation time was something I enjoyed and all those things included in the work of the priesthood.

In the priesthood you start out as an associate, and in those days and it was normal to remain in that position for at least seven years before you could even think about being a pastor. And you're always subjected to whoever that tyrant called "the pastor" was.

My first assignment was unforgettable. That was in 1962. When I met the pastor he said hello and then proceeded to tell me, "You will offer Mass at the missions on Sunday and at the nursing home for the sisters. You will hear confessions. And then you will paint the church and you'll take care of mowing the lawn and the cemetery, and that's all you're going to do." I thought he was joking. I went to my room and found three pages of rules: when you come in, when you go out, where you go, and who you can talk to. There was absolutely no invitation or inclusion of marriages, or instruction for those entering the church, or youth programs, etc. Literally, he meant it. I said Mass on Sundays and weekdays at the manor and then at the two missions.

Whenever I went out the door, he questioned me, "Where are you going?" "Who are you going to see?" "Who did you see?" "What did you talk about?" It was like that for one entire year. It was my first introduction to the priesthood. It was a real letdown as to what really the priesthood should be.

Then, in comes the next guy whom I'm under for four more years. I'm out mowing the lawn in the cemetery, and he drives up. He's not dressed in clerics, he's in shorts. So far as I'm concerned he's just some guy visiting a grave. I don't know.

He said, "Shut that damn thing off."

"Excuse me?" I said.

"Shut that off," he yelled and I shut it off.

"What is that you want?"

He answered, "I'm the new pastor here."

I said, "Oh, my God. Not another tyrant."

He burst out laughing. He turned out to be a wonderful pastor to be under as a young priest. He taught me how to do things the way you should, whether it was instructions or other church matters. You need that as a young priest, to know when to be patient and when not to be patient and when the rules are rules, but sometimes you have to have some consideration. He turned the complete youth program over to me, which I loved.

That was my real introduction to the priesthood. When everything was going really well, on the first of December the bishop called and told me I was being moved to a town on the Canadian border with an old monsignor. And I was going right away. I know nothing about this new place and the only thing I know about the guy I'm going to work with is he's an old guy who spends all his time in the café downtown and doesn't want to bother with the work of a priest.

That is exactly what it was and he was a normal French monsignor. When I got up there he told me to do what needed to be done. If I needed him, he'd be down at the café. He spent all day downtown and came home at night. I'd tell him there were calls for him and he always told me to take care of them, I could handle them. So here I am, in a totally new environment, now practically pastor in context, and I'm trying to do this without any authority.

Ambassadors of the

I decided to visit with our seminarian in Fargo. After a visit you always had to stop at the rector's office to pay a courtesy call. He told me he wanted me here at the seminary in June, to teach. I told him I hadn't taught school. I got out of college with a minor in education and I was so glad to be done with books and school. He told me he knew that, but I had been appointed Youth Director of the diocese in my previous assignment. I had worked with the diocese and the youth programs and developed a number of programs. I didn't think I could do this, but he told me I could take a couple refresher courses during the summer.

So I went there and everything was appalling. I was absolutely terrified. I didn't know what I was doing and I was trying, but I had no idea whether it was working. But it did, it worked extremely well, and I was there fourteen years. I taught English, religion, and Latin. I taught for twenty-nine years.

Into the fifth year the rector was serving as the superintendent in the high school. He told me he was going to send me to school to get a master's degree in education because he wanted me to become the superintendent. I told him, "If you're talking master's you're talking about getting through physics and calculus! The last thing in the world I could ever do was math." He said, "They'll help you get through it."

This is the Call process going on again. Because the rector was going to be leaving, they needed somebody to take over the high school. I ended up for the next eight years as the superintendent.

I had a number of other positions before I received another Calling. I thoroughly got into teaching and enjoyed the whole thing and was having a great time. As always, as soon as I'm enjoying the position, the bishop calls. I'd been there seven years and they always think in terms of changing. The bishop wanted me to be the rector of St. Joseph Cathedral in Sioux Falls, South Dakota. There's this long pause. I'm thinking to myself, *what in the world did he say?* I was a teacher and I had only been in small parishes, nothing big, and he's saying I was to be the rector of the Cathedral! He told me the other pastors in the area said I should come. He said, "I need your answer and I need it to be yes."

That's how I became the rector of the Cathedral. And then, of course, retirement came along.

But I'd like to emphasize that it's always the Call, and at the most inconvenient time the Call changes.

One of my students from forty years ago climbed the corporate ladder with Exxon and was in Houston. I visited him every four years. The year before I retired he asked me where I was retiring to, and I told him Florida. I'd investigated it for three full years to the point where I almost had the house located. He asked whether I'd ever considered Texas and I told him no way because it's too hot and muggy. He took me to Fredericksburg, and then after I examined everything, I ended up in Kerrville where I live now. The cultural aspects of it and the friendliness of the people, that's what eventually got me to settle here.

I went to the Chamber of Commerce to get that yearly calendar and I saw all the things that go in Kerrville. I saw the theater and I visited the beautiful, magnificent church. Somebody told me there was a Catholic high school here and I said to myself, that'd be interesting too.

I wondered about my decision. As a priest, why was I in Kerrville even though I was retired? I had no intention of being here because I didn't know anyone. It was ridiculous.

Well, after spending some time doing my own landscaping and getting acquainted with my neighbors I happened to read in the local newspaper about the good things happening at the Catholic Regional High School which is called Our Lady of the Hills. They were runner up in academics, playoffs in sports, and state titles in the district. That was very exciting, so I decided to visit the school. The principal was on a retreat with the kids, so the secretary showed me around the school. I was not dressed as a priest, but as I was leaving she asked if I was priest. I told her I was but I was retired.

I received a phone call from the principal shortly after that visit. He wanted to take me out to lunch and explain the history of the school and I think some other matters. Well, another Calling came to me. Before I knew it I was saying Mass at the school, meeting the students, saying prayers at the football games, including the road trips and getting home at 3:30 in the morning, giving a blessing at the Honor Society meetings, giving prayers at the Martin Luther King meeting, and many other events. I love it and it is a great place to be because it is not work. And the students need it.

That word Calling is a key word. How many times can you say no and not feel guilty?

It has been a good life. Many people from North and South Dakota ask me why in the world would anybody move to Texas? I tell them, "The people are wonderful. If you want paradise then come to Kerrville because you have terrific people, a God-and-country town where faith is literally lived, not just something they're a part of, beautiful weather, fascinating scenery. I don't know what else you can ask for."

The importance of the dignity of the individual and the relationship are key factors. It's the hardest thing to sell to young people in terms of looking at it as a lifetime. But it's the thing they work at so viciously all the time. My philosophy is the only thing that's ever mattered all the time is family and relationships, friendships, associations, and the dignity of the individual. If there is one thing I try to convince those kids it's to remember: Money is wonderful, power is wonderful, but in the end, the only thing people ever talk about at funerals is how good that person was to them and what that person did for them. This tells us that what matters in life is being there for people. In one word: service. I live in a community that's built around service. I am really blessed to live in Kerrville. When you go out here, remember the most important thing in life will be serving others. And when you do that, everything comes back to you.

Texas is so much more than I ever thought it would be. You always hear about the Texas blowhard and how big Texas is. In terms of people and love for each other, kindness and goodness, Texas is absolutely on top and Kerrville is on top of that.

Ambassadors of the

Donna Schloss

Kerrville, Texas–Minneapolis, Minnesota

I lived in Minnesota until third grade. I was in Minneapolis until I was about three years old, and then lived in the Bemidji area. We then moved to Aurora, Colorado, near Denver, and stayed there until the middle of my senior year in high school. Then we moved to Richardson, Texas because my father's job took him there. He was a salesman and, in spite of my protestations, they took me there.

I don't remember much about my early life except that my first brother was born when I was seven and my second brother was born when I was ten. As a teen, I had a lot of family responsibility as the oldest child and the oldest girl child and the big sister. I started babysitting for neighbors for money when I was about eleven. When I was fourteen, I worked in the cafeteria for my lunch and I worked in the library after school. On weekends I answered phones in a neighbor's beauty shop and did babysitting. At that time, my mother went back to work in the evening, so I was responsible for fixing dinner for my dad and two brothers.

Because I entered Richardson High School at mid-year, I only had a short time to make friends and try to study hard and complete my education. Following high school I went to Texas Women's University in Denton, Texas. I majored in nursing and spent my first year and first summer on the Denton campus, and then did my clinical work at Parkland Hospital in Dallas.

I did many things during my career. I was a junior student at Parkland Hospital when President Kennedy was shot. They took over our classrooms for pressrooms. They also took nursing service for the government office. It was a very interesting and exciting time.

After I graduated from college I worked a year in the emergency room at Parkland in Dallas. Then I went to Europe as a tourist, where I spent three months traveling. During that time I found a civil service job at the American Army Hospital in Heidelberg, Germany, and spent about two years in Europe. While I was in Europe I did a lot of traveling. I went through quite a bit of Western Europe, England, Switzerland, France, Italy, the Netherlands, and Denmark.

I fell in love with an American fellow I met in Europe and we came back to the States. I went to Galveston and worked for six months in the hospital there in what was then a combined intensive care unit. Then I moved to Houston because that's where the man I'd met lived, but pretty quickly thereafter we broke up. I stayed in Houston for several years and worked in the cardiovascular intensive care unit at the Michael DeBakey Medical Center. I worked in the emergency room at Ben Taub General Hospital and also the operating room at Texas Heart Institute with Denton Cooley.

During that time my father died. I felt I needed to get away for a while. I have to backtrack a moment. My parents had found out that the Department of State had nurses overseas and I was interested in traveling. So, I obtained all the paperwork and sent it in. I received a letter back saying thank you very much but positions were frozen, to write back in three months. I wrote back in three months and received no answer. I then found a job opportunity in the Virgin Islands in St. Croix doing public health and off I went. I was there about two years.

I loved the Virgin Islands. However, I was not fond of doing public health work. I found it very interesting, but soon they began having racial problems in St. Croix and several people were killed on a golf course, right in the middle of my public health area. A good friend of mine died and that was very trau-

Ambassadors of the

matic. But I loved the Virgin Islands because it was a great place and the people were wonderful.

My next trip was either meant to be or it was serendipity. I had come back to Texas for Thanksgiving and the holidays. I then returned to St. Croix because I was active in a theater group. At several of the places I went, people said I should call friends of mine that I knew from the theater group. These friends had been talking to a person who was in St. Croix for the holidays, and this person happened to be the Foreign Programs Medical Representative with the Department of State—and they were looking for nurses. This was the very place to which I had previously applied and not gotten an answer.

I was able to get the representative's name and phone number and called him in December. All the paperwork was received. I filled it out and sent it back after the first of the year. At the end of February, I flew to Washington for an interview. My mother, knowing I didn't have a coat, met me at the airport with a coat. In June I started with the State Department and in August 1973 I was in Afghanistan.

It was an amazing place to be at that time. I was in Kabul at the embassy. We had a health unit, which was actually on the compound. There was one stop light in all of Kabul—the capital city. Many of the roads were dirt and the camel caravans came through twice a year up into the mountains and down into the valley. It was a wonderful, fascinating, and magical place to be. I spent a little over two years there.

People were very nice then, but I guess things have changed. From what I hear from a friend who goes back regularly it is different now. Women mostly wore the chadors, but underneath they might be wearing their miniskirts, which were in fashion at the time. There were women teachers and doctors at that time. As Western women, we dressed modestly, but didn't wear the complete coverings. We usually wore long-sleeved shirts and we could wear jeans—that was not a problem. We were able to travel freely and I drove all over the country, including through the Khyber Pass. We used to go from Kabul to Peshawar to go shopping on long weekends. So I drove frequently through the Khyber Pass to Bamiyan where the Buddhists were at the Band-e Amir Lakes. I had many fascination experiences and also took many photographs. I have gone through some of them, but that is what I will do when I retire.

After Afghanistan, I traveled to Cameroon as a medical provider in the embassies. I did all the health and medical care for the U.S. Government where I was. I also evaluated local practitioners and facilities to determine to what extent we could use them. I reported on things that happened in the country that had medical ramifications as well as developing health and medical plans for people there. I was there for two years.

Although I moved around a lot, I enjoyed the different places and their uniqueness. And they were unique then because television wasn't everywhere. Cultures were their own cultures—they hadn't begun to homogenize.

I guess I served as an ambassador from the United States. Many people asked where I was from and it was great being from Texas because everyone knew of

Texas! They all had something to say. Many of them asked about cowboys and Indians. When I first went to Europe, I used to tell people that even I rode a horse to work. Even today in the United States, people come to this area of Texas and they are pretty surprised that it's not flat and dry.

From Cameroon, I came back to the States for a year and did my nurse practitioner work at the University of California in San Diego. From there I went to Somalia where I spent two years and had a wonderful time. Somalia was a very poor country—65 percent of the population were nomads with their camels and goats. The people were friendly. A group of us would camp on the beach on weekends. It was completely safe with no problems and we all had a wonderful time.

When I was there the people really liked Americans. They had just gotten rid of the Russians, but the Americans maintained a diplomatic level in Somalia. There was a decrease in Americans in Ethiopia but an increase of Americans in Somalia. The Americans were just becoming a presence in Somalia, coming in with aid programs and things like that.

With all my international travel and experiences I am not terribly comfortable talking in front of groups of people. I consider myself a shy person and sort of reserved. I don't know why I feel this way. When I was doing public health in the Virgin Islands, I did not enjoy going to the homes of people and presenting myself as somebody who had the answers to their problems. But I was very fortunate working with them when they came to the clinics. One-on-one is fine. It's easy when people come to me, but it is not easy for me to go to someone else.

When I was with the State Department they sent me from Somalia to China and then China to Karachi, Pakistan. As a Foreign Service medical person I provided health and medical care to the U.S. Government. Beijing was fascinating. I think I said that about every country I visited. When I got there in early 1982 everybody still wore their little Mao suits in blue or gray, brown, and beige. There was no color and everything was quite regimented. By the time I left two and a half years later, we were beginning to at least see the children dressed in colors. There was more tourism and things were beginning to loosen up a bit. While there I did some traveling to Tibet.

I was then off to the consulate in Karachi, Pakistan. It was a very interesting time for me. When I arrived, I was the only healthcare provider in Karachi. Several people who were posted in Karachi had been traveling on a plane that was hijacked and landed in Teheran. I think it was the Saudi Airlines, but I am not sure. We didn't know what would happen. I was sitting with one of the families watching CNN, which we could get at that time, and they saw their husband/father get shot at the top of the stairs of the plane and tumble to the bottom.

That was how I started my tour in Karachi. Working with them and the whole community was difficult when dealing with this trauma. The end of my tour in Karachi came with the hijacking of the Pan-Am plane at the airport in Karachi. The hijackers set off some grenades and started machine-gunning some of the passengers. I had a lot to do after that. I did everything from pulling shrapnel out of a person's butt to coordinating with the Air Force the med-evac of all the people from the Western hemisphere. Finding and visiting with them in different hospitals, determining what kind of support they would need, getting them from the hospitals to the planes, and determining what they would need on the planes was hectic. I also had to determine in one case that somebody was not going to make it and could not be evacuated. But, in another instance, I was able to find a mother and a child who were in two different hospitals. Both thought the other was dead and it was a real joy to unite them.

From Pakistan I went to Rome, Italy and I was there for four years. What's not to like about Italy? I gained fifteen pounds! I really loved it there. I learned enough of the language to have some basic conversations. It was the same in all the countries. I could shop, get food, find a place to stay, ask for a toilet, and have some of the niceties. Except for China where I could not read or write, I had just some of the basic words.

From Italy I went to Nicaragua and from there to Madagascar. Madagascar was my final place and I retired out of there. I also did short-term assignments in Sarajevo, Bosnia, Jakarta, Indonesia, and Rabat, Morocco. I took an early retirement and couldn't work for the government for about five years.

My family—my mother and my two younger brothers—lived in the Dallas area when I was getting ready to retire. I wanted to be relatively close to my family. Even though Texas is big compared to the places I'd been, this was relatively close. I was going to look for a place to retire on my home leave out of Nicaragua. I had almost three months, but two weeks before I was due to come back to Texas my mother went into the hospital with terminal cancer. So I spent those three months with her.

I'd been through this area a lot, and I knew people in Texas retired to Kerrville. It just happened that I ran into someone who was beginning to develop this garden home area, which I felt would meet my needs. I found I could afford to live in Kerrville, which was a big surprise to me. I bought a lot—the money went into escrow because they weren't ready yet to sell lots. They didn't even have roads into the area at that time.

Then I went back to Nicaragua, and from Nicaragua to Madagascar. I came back from Madagascar to do continuing education in Baltimore. I flew down for a week, with a three-day weekend, and I got a bank loan, found a builder, designed the house, picked out all the appliances, the flooring, the fence, everything for the house in that week, before I went back to Madagascar. I came back to Texas the first of January of 1996, and moved in.

I felt retirement meant you did the things you thought needed to be done instead of what somebody else thought you should be doing. I wanted to work in a free clinic, and I wanted to do some disaster relief. So, as a volunteer, I began doing disaster relief with the American Red Cross. I do disaster mental health with the Red Cross. I have gone out on many disasters. The American Red Cross covers the Territories, so I went to Guam with them for three weeks. It was after a big typhoon

I have been to tornados in Texas and floods in California. Tornados in Florida and hurricanes in Florida. I was on-call for the aviation incident response team in September of 2001. I was on the earliest flight out of the San Antonio airport to go to New York. We couldn't fly into New York, so we flew into Philadelphia and went by train into New York City. I did disaster mental health after the World Trade Center attack. I was there for two weeks, and then I went back in November for two weeks.

It was a very difficult time. There was a lot of sadness and things that happened that couldn't be explained. People trying to learn to deal with loss—all disasters are that way. It doesn't matter if you've lost your loved ones in the World Trade Center attack or in a hurricane or tornado. Loss is still the same. But the magnitude of it was pretty horrendous.

Coping with the stress of the situation can be difficult. One of the things the Red Cross did was establish a disaster mental health element of the American Red Cross to provide some support to the relief workers who found themselves constantly being re-exposed to trauma. I guess you work through it with your friends, knowing what's normal and knowing the processes of grieving and dealing with things like this.

A week before this happened, I had come home from my shift at the Museum of Western Art in Kerrville and found that my dog that I had rescued had gotten her collar tangled in the patio table and had strangled. This was the Tuesday before 9/11. When I came back from 9/11 I felt I needed a companion—I was not ready for an attachment, but knew there were animals that needed homes. So I went to all of the Humane Societies and SPCAs and pounds, and found three dogs I liked, and took the one that had been incarcerated the longest. Now I have my beloved Misha. I've had her since October of 2001.

I still do relief service. Well, the Red Cross was retirement. That's volunteering. Retirement wasn't about not working, it just meant I stopped being paid. I seem to volunteer quite a bit. I have volunteered at the Museum of Western Art. I do some volunteer things for Kerrville Art and Cultural Center. I volunteer for CASA, Court Appointed Special Advocates for children in the court system. I do their adoption home studies. I do disaster relief and other things with the American Red Cross. I was, for a period of time, the medical officer for our Civil Air Patrol squadron here. Of course, like everybody else in Kerrville, I do things for my church. I seem to be busy! Oh, I forgot the big one. I volunteer every Monday at the Raphael Free Community Clinic. I see patients there. And I've done some volunteer work for the Humane Society.

I do have some free time, but rarely. Somebody gave me T-shirt for Christmas that said, "Stop me before I volunteer again."

What kind of legacy would I like to leave the young people of our country and the world? I think maybe tolerance is a good word. Compassion and tolerance. Hopefully, people can open their eyes to the needs beyond themselves, and view the world with compassion and tolerance.

Ambassadors of the

Hans Schlunegger

Kerrville. Texas–Zurich. Switzerland

My name is Hans Willie, Hans for short, and I immigrated from Zurich, Switzerland in 1959. First we went to Seattle, Washington and we lived there for three years. We then moved here in '62 because we just couldn't resist coming to Texas—we couldn't wait to get to Texas. It's a beautiful state and people are exceptionally friendly. It's a good place to raise your kids and I wouldn't go anywhere else. In Europe, Texas was *the* state of the United States.

We ended up in Houston first because Houston had opportunities for a chef, which I was. We were there for seven years and the time had come for us to try to reach the American dream. The way you do that is by becoming self-employed, becoming your own boss. We had an opportunity in Kerrville to start our own business. We took that opportunity and moved here in 1969. The opportunity for self-employment was number one, and number two, well, where else would you want to raise kids besides Kerrville? There's just no other place in the world.

We hadn't heard about Kerrville before we arrived—it was new to me and when the opportunity arose we traveled to Kerrville. We immediately fell in love with the community. The people were exceptionally nice and received us as though we had known each other forever. I had a job offer in Los Angeles at one time. It paid twice as much as what we earned in Texas, but no dice, against the protest of my wife.

When I was a child we lived in a small community outside of Zurich and this was during the World War II. Even though Switzerland was not directly involved with the war, we were rationed and food was short. We watched the American bombers fly over our little city and land in Dusseldorf. It was an exciting time for us kids.

We would leave home in the morning and come home for lunch at noon and be gone again all day until it was time to have supper. And nobody cared, nobody worried about us. It was really, really a beautiful time for us.

I hated school—I was just not a school person. I prevailed in sports including gymnastics and swimming, as well as singing and music. But anything else I couldn't care less about. It was the same with high school. I didn't care for it or for the teacher we had. We had a man teacher who ran the class for all the subjects. I didn't like him and he didn't like me. Even so, I passed every semester and never had to stay back. I was pretty mediocre in my grades. School was not something I enjoyed at all, but today I probably would. But not at that time.

I finished high school at sixteen. I immediately took a job in the French part of Switzerland where I managed to learn the French language. It was a small community and I was working for a farmer who had maybe ten acres of vineyards. I was there for a whole year, away from home—I didn't see my parents for a whole year. I came back home again when I was almost seventeen.

I was very much involved in sports in high school and after I left school. I was very good in sports and was always in the top two or three. I played some football, which was really soccer, and I was very good in swimming. I really enjoyed diving and swimming. But I also enjoyed music. We had a very good music teacher and I enjoyed that very much. I had a good voice at that time so I sang in the choir.

After high school it was difficult to attend the university or college because only people who had the money could go. Out of our class of about twenty-five or thirty, only two went to college. One of them became an electrical engineer and another became a teacher. We took an apprenticeship and I chose to become a cook. I made cook's apprenticeship in Basel, which is a border city between Germany, France, and Switzerland. It was an exciting time in a beautiful city. Doing the cook's apprenticeship meant I went to what would be equal to a college. And I had to pass that in order to get my grade as a cook finally.

The apprenticeship itself is two and a half years and then there's another half-year where you kind of transform into becoming a real cook. You build yourself up from one station to the next, from people who make the vegetables, then the people who do meat, then those who make the sauces, the soups, and the pastry.

You have to learn in each station until you become an expert in it. Then you move to the next one.

Becoming a cook was my father's suggestion. My mother wanted me to become a reporter. I was pretty good at writing in school—that's one thing I enjoyed. But my father said, "Son, if you're a cook you never have to worry about where the next meal comes from." He had a point, but you have to remember that after World War II things were not very rosy. It was very tough to make a living and very hard to get a job. I think I chose the right profession because I was a natural at it. I have always enjoyed it, even though my wife is the better cook.

My wife is a fascinating person. We met in hotel school, which was part of college. She was the first in her family to have a higher education. One thing led to another and we eventually got to know each other closer. At that time she was engaged with someone else, which made it feasible for her to attend school. At the end of school she moved in with my parents where she became a waitress. My parents had a restaurant in the little town where I grew up and we just grew very close together. We got married a year after we left school.

You progress to become a better and better cook. Your position grows until you become an assistant to the executive chef and then you eventually become an executive chef. I was a chef already in Europe and I was running a kitchen by myself. Then I came to America to live in Seattle. I worked at the Olympic Hotel in Seattle, which at that time was the best international hotel. It was a big hotel with a huge crew. I started out at the very bottom, doing soups and sauces, and after about six months I was already a station chef.

I grew higher and by the time I left I was a chef on my own. I had an offer to go Los Angeles to open two hotels for Hyatt. At that time, all they had were airport hotels. I had another offer to go to Houston to work at the Rice Hotel. I thought I wasn't ready for the Hyatt job, even though they paid twice as much as the job in Houston. AnneMarie, my wife, would've loved to have gone to Los Angeles. We had such good friends in Seattle. She didn't want to go that far away, I think that was part of it. But also the money was important. When we started out in America I made so little money that we barely got by. We had one son at that time whom we brought over with us and we immediately had a daughter. So we were pretty strung out. I think money was part her willingness to go to Los Angeles.

But my mind was made up and I wanted to go to Texas. So I ended up at the Rice Hotel as assistant to the executive chef. Then the job at the Warwick Hotel opened up. The owner said I was the right chef for him because I had the knowledge as well as the enthusiasm to make it a truly wonderful hotel. And really, it was a great, great hotel, the Warwick. I stayed with them for five years.

That's when I started to think about my future because I believed I'd come to the top of my career. By the time I left there I was in charge of all food and beverage operations for the whole company. I was in Acapulco for several weeks helping them take over three hotels there.

When I came back home I knew I had to be my own entrepreneur. I started to inquire about places when a local lady by the name of Naomi Ingram, who was associated with Kerrville Chamber of Commerce, talked about the Inn of the Hills and the beautiful Angora Club there. I went to see it and I fell in love with the setting. The Inn of the Hills was truly a number one, first class hotel at the time, 1969.

We made a contract for three years that I would take over the food operation and the bar and the club. I worked for eighteen hours a day with no days off. But we eventually became successful and the last twelve months we really started to make good money. We built our house here and started to reach the American dream. Then the owner sold the hotel and the new owners wanted to move in another direction.

I looked further and we found the Sunday House being built where I-10 comes through now, and they made me an offer to lease the restaurant from them. The owner, Mr. Parker, was an exceptional businessman and he knew how to make money. That's what inspired me a little, watching what he was doing.

He offered us a hotel for sale in Ruidoso, New Mexico and without hesitation I said yes. We purchased the hotel knowing we would lose a lot of money in the beginning. We then built a discotheque across from the Sunday House— discotheques were fashionable in the seventies. We made good money there and the money helped us to operate the Swiss Chalet in Ruidoso. We held on to the hotel there, rebuilding it as we went along and making it more and more up to date. We had it for twenty-five years before we sold it.

Meanwhile, we had purchased two hotels in West Texas, the Sunday House in Fort Stockton and the Sunday House in Pecos. We operated there for several years. We worked very hard and it looked like we were going to make it when the bottom fell out with oil business in 1986. It was almost like starting over from square one. It was very hard to get back on our feet.

Texas is such a big state that if you want to have multiple restaurants or hotels you have to fly between points. So I got my pilot's license in the early '70s and bought my first airplane—I still have an airplane today. I traveled back and forth, especially to Ruidoso, by airplane.

Our children were growing up in Kerrville, of course. They stuck with us all the way through high school when they decided to work for us. We had plenty of hotels now for them to take over in management or sublevel management, like running the kitchen, running the bar, as well as the restaurant. Willy, our oldest son, did all our renovations. He has a degree from Texas University in Austin in structural engineering. He built the new hotel in Pecos for us.

I have three children. Willy was born in Zurich, Switzerland. He was a very bright young boy from the very beginning. We came to America in '59 when he was sixteen months old. He went to school here, of course, in America. He's always had grades that were very satisfactory. Early on he had the talent for doing things with his hands. He built a bar and nailed it together with roofing nails.

Willy went to UT and we helped with money and got him a car, but he actually earned his own way to go to college. He worked himself through

Ambassadors of the

because we, at that time, were not rich people. So the children had to attend to themselves pretty much. He was at Schreiner for about a year, too. So were the other children, Marion and Kurt. They went to hotel school at the University of Houston.

Kurt, the youngest, is still working with us as the general manager in Pecos where he takes care of both hotels. He got married and they have three children. Marion, who worked with us at the Inn of the Hills, like all the other children did, is still working at the Inn in the sales department. She's a delightful young lady and has two children. Unfortunately, her first marriage didn't work out, but she is now engaged with a nice young man, kind of opposite to the first one. He's more of the cowboy type, a real down-to-earth kind of guy, very helpful to her.

There was a time when AnneMarie and I worked many hours. At one time AnneMarie was running the Alpine Lodge Restaurant near the Sunday House all by herself, and that was a big, big operation, a huge business. I must say I've never seen an individual who was capable of running such an operation and be so profitable. If it wasn't for her and what she was able to accomplish there I don't know if we would've survived some of the crises we had. She's a top-notch executive.

I love to play the piano, and now that I'm not tied up with business I try to play two hours a day, every day. I also enjoy writing. My first book is about some experiences I had while I was in the military—the military is required for Swiss people. I enjoyed writing this book and I had many interesting experiences in between. My second book is about our life story, how we met and then immigrated to the United States, as well as starting our hotel business.

I would say there's no such substitute for hard work and integrity. I think it comes at a cost today. My final words? Enjoy the read, but take it with a grain of salt.

John Vece

Kerrville, Texas–Chicago, Illinois

I was born in Chicago, Illinois in 1938, and I lived and worked there for forty-two years. My mother and father were both from fairly large families. We lived in an Italian area in Chicago, and I had plenty of relatives nearby. Much of my young life was spent within the family and family affairs.

My mother was born in Chicago. A couple of her older sisters were born in Italy—she came from a family of eleven. Both sides of the family immigrated from a small town in the southern part of Italy not far from Salerno. The two

Ambassadors of the

families knew each other, and that's how my mother and father got together. I guess they always knew each other.

My Grandpa Pete was a barber. My grandma on my mother's side died about six years before I was born. She was kind of a flapper from that era and worked at Western Electric, an old AT&T subsidiary. My father came to this country when he was about six, I believe. My grandfather had come here and was working on the railroad, and saved enough money to bring the family over. My father went to work after grade school in a clothing factory making men's suits. He worked in that place for fifty years.

My father got drafted into the Army in 1944. To help make ends meet, my mother went to work at small factories around our neighborhood. She worked in one that made model airplane kits, and later she worked in a bindery where they put books together. They always went to work, and they always sent us to school. My brother and I both had excellent attendance records because our parents would chase us out the door.

My parents retired to a nice little home in the southern suburbs of Chicago. My father passed away about seven years ago at the age of ninety-two. My mother passed away three years ago, and she made it to ninety-four, so I may have a few years ahead of me based on those genetics.

I had a rather easy time of it at school. I was advanced two grades. I'm not sure if it was because I was smart or because they were just trying to make room for the all the Baby Boomers coming in behind me. I was a reader. I frequented the library. Academics were no problem, but I wasn't going to a college preparatory school either. I was poorly coordinated, so I didn't get involved much in sports. I finally got coordinated enough to bowl, and did fairly well. I wound up acting as the secretary, keeping tabs of the scores, team standings, and all that.

I went to Chicago Vocational High School, where I was gearing toward the foundry trade. Otherwise, I took all the standard courses. I made some friends early in high school, and pretty much stayed with them the whole four years. I've continued those relationships up to today. One of those friends stayed at our house a couple months ago.

My father and uncle owned the small apartment building where we lived. Although I wasn't too proficient with my hands, as I got older, whenever my father wanted me to do something—like painting or shoveling coal for our boiler—I did it.

I went to work in a foundry for a while. I aspired to something more, so I started to take some college preparatory courses because I couldn't get admitted to college immediately with my background. I did all right.

A funny thing happened on the way. I got very interested in my church, and wound up going into the seminary for three years. I had two years of college in the seminary. It was a very rewarding experience, but I came to realize that being a priest was not something I could do well. When I came out of there, the Cuban Missile Crisis was heating up so I went into the Army. I spent my time in Germany, and I took some correspondence courses to continue my college education.

When I came out of the Army, I got a job as an accountant and I went to night school to finish my degree in accounting. I specialized in the tax area. After getting my bachelor's degree in accounting, I received a master's degree in taxation, which was a relatively new program at that time. I received both degrees from DePaul University in Chicago. I worked in the tax department, or managed tax departments, for forty years.

I started out working for a building materials handling company, Vulcan Materials. After a few years, I went to one of their competitors, Materials Service in Chicago, and worked in their tax department for about seven years. I got involved in the Chicago Tax Club, which was a group of tax executives and managers, to try to build up my experience and learn from people I admired greatly. They really knew their stuff and I learned a lot from them that helped me do a better a job.

I realized I could only go so far with those particular companies, and took a managerial position with a trucking company. There was a lot of restructuring going on in the trucking industry, and in order to survive, they merged with another company here in Texas. The company moved me down here, and I thought it was a wonderful experience. Unfortunately, they weren't able to survive all the turmoil in the industry. I wound up going to work for an HMO after my company went bankrupt. The company was in Dallas, and I lived in the suburbs. I worked with the HMO for five or six years until they relocated to the Northeast.

Because of my family situation with the kids in school, I decided to stick around. Plus, I liked Texas. I went to work for another trucking company in the Dallas area. I worked there several years until, with continuing turmoil in the economy, they relocated. At that point, I was active in another tax organization, the Tax Executives Institute, and had met quite a few people. I got the opportunity to move to a very stable company, Frito Lay, which was a subsidiary of PepsiCo. I finished the final ten years of my career there. I was always doing something in the taxes, and the taxes just kept growing, so there was more to do.

I still do my family taxes and the reports to the Internal Revenue Service for the Alpha Omega Center. I have a license to practice before the IRS, which I maintain with the necessary amount of continuing education. But I haven't gotten actively involved in having a business. There are other fellows out there who need to make a living—I'm content to help in specific areas without going into competition.

Once I retired, I never considered going back up north. My second wife is originally from San Antonio. She's familiar with the Hill Country. When it came time for retirement, she said, "We're going to move to the Hill Country," and I said, "Okay, where is it?" We looked throughout the Canyon Lake area, Boerne, Fredericksburg, and Kerrville. We found a place we really liked in Kerrville, and it's just been an upward track. I keep finding more things that I like about Kerrville the longer I'm here. Some of our family and friends wondered why we did not return to the north. When they came to visit, they understood pretty well why I'm not interested in returning!

Besides the fact that in January I didn't have to wear twenty layers of clothing, I liked the political atmosphere here. After growing up in Chicago with—I don't know a good euphemism for the kind of politics that occurred up there—the politics here seemed more honest and open, and that I liked. I liked the people. I had an interesting experience in Dallas when I was still working. I was talking to a young lady and I said I really like the small town atmosphere here (I was talking about Dallas). Coming from Chicago, Dallas was a small metropolis. She gave me a funny look because she was from a town of about 300 people in East Texas, and she had no clue what I was talking about!

Frankly, I think I've gotten more out of Texas than I've put in. But I've tried to help out wherever I could. I'm active in the Knights of Columbus. I'm helping out with Youth Ministry at Notre Dame Church, teaching catechism to the seventh and eighth graders from public school. I'm working with the Alpha Omega Life Center, which is our local pregnancy center. It's a pro-life group that I'm pretty involved in, and I'm acting as treasurer. I have a fourteen-year-old son enrolled in Notre Dame School, and have gotten pulled into the activities of the school, the Parent-Teacher Club, and I'm acting as treasurer there. I also serve as president of our Homeowners' Association in Northwest Hills. So, I'm a little busy, trying to help, trying to make Texas as nice a place as I found it, and maybe a little better.

I used to be into model railroading. Coming from Chicago, the railroad center of the country, that kind of got into me. I've drifted away from that, but I still maintain a lot of interest in railroads and subscribe to magazines to keep up on what's going on in the industry.

As to the future, I still have a young boy to get through school. He'll be starting high school in the fall, so I'm still eight or ten years away from getting him through the whole education process—if we can keep him interested in education that long. Video games seem to be a big distraction for him.

I can't remember the exact book in the Bible, but one talks about a man's legacy being his children. I have a son and daughter, and after many false starts, especially on my son's part, both of them are doing quite well. Their lives are going along very well. Judy has three children, two of them are doing very well, and the third one we're still working on. And we've got Skylar, fourteen years old, and we're trying to set an example for him. Not only through ourselves, but through the other children in the family. My father's philosophy was, if the children are good and successful—not so much in monetary terms, but in terms of living happy lives—that's the main accomplishment you can have in your life.

If I was with a group of young people, I would tell them to look for good role models. Use them for examples. I have had dozens of role models in my life and I picked out various qualities they had and tried to imitate them. That is the biggest thing I can say.

LLANO

Ambassadors of the

Elizabeth Hayes, Stay-at-Home Mom

Llano, Texas–Richmond, Indiana

Be honest with yourself and start dancing at an early age.

Frank Rowell

Llano, Texas–Marlboro, Massachusetts

I was born in Marlboro, Massachusetts and raised in Nashua, New Hampshire. I was there until I was about twenty years old. After that, I lived in Colorado and then New Mexico for about twenty-five years, before coming to Llano about twelve years ago.

Ambassadors of the

My attraction to Llano was primarily business. New Mexico was very difficult place to eke out a living. I worked numerous fairs and festivals throughout Texas over the years and Llano seemed to be centrally located to where I was earning a living. I selected Llano specifically because I wanted a hilly terrain— flat country didn't appeal to me. I wrote letters to every city and town in the Hill Country; Llano answered my letters and kept sending materials, this was a spot that deserved looking into.

I asked about the community, what was here, what the tourism was like, and what it would be like to move a business here. They responded with lots of information about the banks and all the happenings here. Other towns didn't provide the information I requested. The Chamber of Commerce was a very positive thing. I am very happy here and I don't think I could've made a better choice.

When I was young, Nashua was a small city and I lived in a very old part of town. It was a working-class neighborhood and I went to a very old elementary school, from the 1800s, and things had not changed much. In fact, I think we still had the principal from then!

I lived near the housing projects in a small house. There were lots of other kids in the area. It was a very quiet and safe area and there was no crime to speak of. When I was a teenager we moved to the neighboring town, Hudson, New Hampshire. It was a small town where we played basketball and football.

I had a small group of friends who stayed in the same neighborhood we grew up in. Most of our parents worked for the same business, a big machine shop. Almost everyone I knew planned to be in that neighborhood their whole lives. When they got through school they knew they would get a job at the machine shop. I still have contact with some of my old buddies and we meet every once in a while.

For many years I traveled and worked fairs in Maine and New Hampshire in the summer. I've been in the jewelry business all my life, ever since I got away from the machine shop where I did work for a while. The jewelry business is a retail business. I was originally based in Colorado when I started. I started with Indian jewelry. I moved to Colorado because I had a cousin who had a campground and RV with cabins just outside of Rocky Mountain National Park. I was there at the time of the big Thompson flood back in the mid-seventies. I spent the summer working for the Red Cross.

I ended up in the jewelry business because the people I was staying with had a jewelry store. I worked for them for about five years. They were with the Blake Jewelry Company. A lot of the jewelry came from the reservations in New Mexico and Arizona. Although I made a little bit of jewelry I mostly sold jewelry. I managed their road operation and did a lot of fairs in Colorado. We also sold jewelry at parking lots and rest areas. I met a number of Indians and learned what sold and how to go about getting a place to sell jewelry. We sold just about everything—rings, bracelets, necklaces, squash blossoms, and concho belts. We also sold rugs and furs.

I did the roadside sales around central Colorado and lower Wyoming. When my wife and I got together, we broke off on our own. Blake Jewelry could no longer provide any further advancement because they were staying a small business with two or three employees. I was totally on my own at that point. We didn't have much of an investment. We had a small amount of silver from my wife's first marriage because her husband made silver jewelry. We traded that in and bought $700 worth of jewelry, and we were in business. I enjoyed travelling for many years and we didn't stay still a whole lot. I've been doing this now for over thirty years. I don't think retirement is something you get to do when you're self-employed. You don't have a retirement plan.

My folks were originally from New England where my father's family settled in 1630. My father's family was pretty much English and everybody in the family was English. No deviation there and they had lived in the same part of New Hampshire since the 1630s. My mother's family was Irish/German and her family had been there, I think, since the 1700s. My dad worked in the machine shop, where we all anticipated we'd end up, and once he got laid off when I was a kid. He and another guy who also got laid off started a company. In his late fifties he discovered I was selling Indian jewelry and he thought that would be fun so he left and started selling Indian jewelry at county fairs and flea markets. He followed me in the same business. He thought it was a lot better than the machine shop.

My mom, when I was real little, worked in a card shop where they made greeting cards. Most of the time while I was growing up, though, she didn't work. She was the one who encouraged my father to do the jewelry because she wanted to do house parties. She did a lot of house parties and sold a lot of jewelry. They did this for about eighteen years. My dad is eighty and he continued to do county fairs and went back and forth to Florida until cancer ended that.

I am very involved in the Llano community. I'm on the Board of Directors for the Chamber of Commerce. I am president of the Main Street Program. I'm also on the Board of Directors for the Red Top Jail and on the Board of Directors for the Llano Community Center. I co-manage the theatre along with the mayor of the city.

People ask me when do I have the time to do all this. I tell them I don't, I make time. When there's an event going on Sunday, I will work Sunday. A lot of the other things are during the week. During my free time I like to go rock hounding and rock collecting. I always enjoyed gold panning in this area. We used to make trips to New Mexico on a regular basis before we opened the store.

While living here, I founded the Main Street Program, which was probably the most important one, with the most benefits to the community. It was through the Texas Historical Commission. It's a national program and we offer grants to businesses to remodel the fronts of their businesses. It's the one that started getting the theatre back in operation again as well as the jail program. We started the program to save the jail from falling apart. I am speaking about the same jail we are sitting in for this interview. You don't see any bars because the cells are upstairs. I believe my contributions have helped to improve the community in which I live and I try to be helpful to organizations as best I can.

Texans have reacted quite well to these efforts. I have been able to fit in here and everybody has been just as nice as can be. I have lived in Llano County for about twelve years. I've had a store here for about five years but during the first few years we traveled a lot and this was our base of operation. We didn't work here.

People come from all over to buy jewelry, but people from all over the world come to buy rocks. They come to my shop to buy rocks because they are recession proof. Local rocks have lots of minerals in them and that was another reason for coming to Llano. This is the center for the gem and mineral area of Texas. Llanite, which I knew nothing about until I got here, is well known all over the world. People come here to buy Llanite and they'll take fifty pounds of it on the plane back to Europe or to Asia.

What do they do with rocks? I think they set them on a table or shelf. Rock collection is a big hobby. Llano is known for being the only place in Texas where you can look for gold. There's gold in the Llano River. People come here from all over Texas to pan for gold.

My legacy to others would be to spend a lot of time thinking about what you want to do. I worked I n the machine shop because I didn't know what I wanted to do. It's taken until I came here to figure out what I wanted to do because it was a hobby. The jewelry was work and the rocks are a hobby. Just find something you enjoy doing and make that what you do in life.

Another factor would be to get involved in your community. Volunteer service is probably the best thing anyone can do. Volunteering is how the world seems to work.

I was in the Volunteer Fire Department for about nine years in New Mexico. I served there as an Assistant Fire Chief for a while. Here, I got started because the Chamber of Commerce dragged me in and it went from one thing to another. Not many people get involved in volunteer work on the same level. I find it very gratifying, especially with the jail because I got in at the beginning and now we're restoring it.

You asked about my moustache, beard, and hair. We do quite a bit of re-enactment-type things and I grew the mustache as part of an Old West event we did here. We have several of them a year and the locals really enjoy them. Right now we're getting ready for the gold-panning event. I will probably be an 1890s prospector. Also, in October we have a beard-growing contest with the Heritage Days. I may get involved in doing that too.

I really enjoy life. Everybody has days when you wonder why you keep doing this. But I enjoy being able to do things that make other people happy and I find it gratifying to be able to keep the theatre open. I'm probably there way too many hours—it seems I am there first thing in the morning and at the end of the day.

Things don't get done unless someone gets out there and does it. This is especially true in a small town. I don't know much about big cities because I've never lived in a big city. But in a small town, most things get done by people who see what needs to be done and they do it. I think all members of the community need to help make their town a better place in which to live.

Ambassadors of the

Raymer Wiese, Cabinetmaker

Llano, Texas–Blueworth, Minnesota

The three things I have tried to live by every day are consideration, honesty, and respect.

MARBLE FALLS

Michael Clark

Marble Falls. Texas–Willard. Ohio

I live in Horseshoe Bay and I work in Marble Falls, and I blow things up for a living. I was born in Willard, Ohio and the first farm we lived on was outside that city. When I was in fourth through fifth grade, the family moved to Boulder, Colorado, then we moved back to northern Ohio in 1970 and lived on a farm until I was in high school. The farm had grains and a small herd of Angus cattle.

In 1976, the family piled into the car and took a trip to Colorado just to visit the stomping grounds. We went through Laramie, Wyoming. There were some pretty small towns in Wyoming and I had lived in small towns my whole life. I really missed being in the mountains while we lived in Colorado, so I went to Wyoming for my college education.

A high school biology teacher, back in Ohio, encouraged me to get a job in geology. The idea was to get rich working in oil. I graduated in Laramie about the time the oil bust hit and the battle cry was if you couldn't get a job, go to grad school. I wanted to anyway, so I went to grad school in Bozeman, Montana and was there for four years.

I worked most of my way through grad school doing summer work with a company mining talcum powder. I actually got paid to hike around the mountains of Montana looking for rocks, which was a great job for a young, budding geologist. I got to work in an underground open pit plant for three years.

I left Montana and got a job with a mining company and I worked in a laboratory in Georgia for six months. From there I went to Los Angeles for two months—same company, different laboratories. I did the same type of work with microscopes and analytical stuff in laboratories. They closed that down and sent some of us to Denver, Colorado for about four months and then transferred me back to Montana. It was great going home again with the same company. I lived there four years and got married in Montana.

One thing led to another and we wound up making a move with the company to Houston, Texas. What a change that was from Montana. In Houston I got divorced and moved to Marble Falls to escape Houston. It was a nice town, but just too big for me as well as hot and humid compared to where I grew up. I discovered Marble Falls in 1999 or 2000 and have been here ever since.

I don't have family in Texas now, but Grandma was born in Greenville, Texas. After Mom and Dad got divorced, Dad visited the San Antonio area. He never talked much about that time down here for a few winters. He may have traipsed some of the same hills that I've traipsed since. He only died about five years ago.

I was attracted to Texas because of the job opportunities. The Horseshoe Bay area gave me a chance to stay in the same industry. I like mining, and friends have told me mining is really a basic industry like farming.

Growing up on a farm as a kid was just great and I wouldn't change it for anything. I believe youngsters who were born in the city would find it hard to live in the country. They'd have a nervous anxiety that would never leave. If you were born in the country, you can always find things to do and be more creative. A country boy can always go to the city and come home. Looking back on it, I very much appreciate the basic grounding I received and the experiences. It may sound strange to somebody else but one of my fondest memories was following behind Dad and the plow looking for earthworms. They came in handy when I went fishing.

It was hands-on learning all the time. We had an old farm that you don't see much anymore. The cows were in the bottom of the barn and hay bales on top. We had hay bale forts in there. I'd swing on ropes from one part of barn to the

Ambassadors of the

other and drop off. This would probably be considered a little unsafe today, but I survived. I was still pretty young but I helped feed cattle and cared for the horses out in the pastures.

I was probably an average student in school from kindergarten to about sixth grade. Then something happened in seventh grade that was pretty profound and I will forever thank my math teacher who was kind of a mentor for me. I was learning how to play chess and it was a big thing for me to finally beat him because he was a math teacher and secretary of the chess club in a nearby town. Looking back on it, I'm sure he let me beat him, just for the confidence experience.

I had finished the school year, in sixth grade. I had gotten the previous week off to help Dad plant corn and I missed the finals in math. It was the week to wrap up the school year. My teacher said, "Mike, you got a high B but you missed the final. I'll make you a deal. You can skip the final if you like and I'll give you the B. Or, take a chance and if you can pass the final, I'll give you an A for the course." My schoolmates said, "Just forget the final, you got it made." Well, I took the final and ended up getting the A. That was a game changer because from then through the rest of high school it was straight As every time. I was really impressed with him and I learned that if you really apply yourself, you can succeed at things.

In high school I wasn't very athletic. I did a lot of Future Farmers of America activities and was in a lot of organizations, but I regret to say that I was shy around girls.

I left home in 1964 in a Ford Falcon van that belonged to the Volunteer Fire Department. Because I was the oldest son going off to college, first to leave the nest, my mother was all teary-eyed. I graduated with a bachelor's degree in geology from the University of Wyoming in Laramie. I went on to receive a master's degree in geology from Montana State University. I have been employed as a geologist since halfway through my master's degree, since 1985.

I'll be happy to explain what I really do in my job. I work for a mining company and we blow up a thousand tons of rock at a time, every morning, underground. We have a machine that drills fifteen-foot holes in a wall, a space that's fifty feet wide by twenty-five feet tall, and it drills a pattern of fifty or sixty holes. Each hole gets filled with dynamite and ammonium nitrate fuel oil. At 5:00 in the morning the blaster ignites the fuel and it blows it up and you end up with 1,000 or 1,500 tons of rubble on the ground.

But the most fun part of all is every so often, I'll get to shut off the shot, "hold the shot" is what they call it. It's no more than a pop like you'd get at a Fourth of July parade, which starts a three-foot-long fuse burning. That burns and you need to be out of there by then because it will ignite the whole blast. You can feel them if you're close enough and you can hear them—it sounds like a roll of distant thunder and it takes about four seconds to go boom, boom, boom. Not all at once, it's easy enough so it's not going to affect the buildings. I don't do that often. I'm really the environmental health and safety guy not the blaster, but every so often I help out.

Some people in the community hear the blasts. If the blasts don't happen at exactly 5:00, some people ask what happened because they didn't get their wake-up call and they may be late for work.

All that rock is removed from underground and we make gravel out of it. We bring that gravel into town and make powder out of it. The powder is used to make paint and wallboard putties and construction putties as well as compounds, PVC pipe, and lots of other construction materials.

My parents were interesting people. Dad was a big man. He was always kind of a quiet person, a carpenter, a farmer, very good with his hands and very good at what he did. He didn't talk much, but he was a hard worker. He was one of a generation of men who did the right things and good things. He never talked a lot with his kids or had deep conversations, except one time when he took me to catch a train back to Wyoming for college and the train was about four or five hours late. I'm glad it was because he opened up about the time he spent in the Korean War and he admitted he wasn't actually in combat but was in Germany during the war.

When they recruited him he told them he wanted to play football. Now, Dad was about six-four, and solid muscle when he was in his prime. He told me he was never afraid of anything or anybody. He played fullback and he would bust through lines and was pretty good in Army football in Germany.

I was impressed by some of the things he used to do. He could put a bundle of shingles on either shoulder and walk up a ladder. Those things are heavy and it would take a lot of stamina and strength to do something like that. When I drove around with him in Ohio on weekends to work on projects or on the farm, he'd point out at different houses or buildings he'd either built or remodeled. It was important to him, and left an impression on me that he could point at something he had done physically and with pride say, "I did that." He had a physical hand in helping erect something for somebody else. It's a monument to yourself and to your profession to be able to do that. I always considered him as a quiet mentor.

My mom was about five-two on a tall day. But she was always a strength to the family too. She worked at a factory in Ohio selling gloves and then came home to raise us kids. Both parents worked and I am very grateful to them for giving us a very good home over the years, in all the different places we lived, then the final family farm in Ohio.

My aunt did some genealogy to find out if we were eligible to be sons and daughters of the American Revolution. We had ancestors on both sides of the Civil War and she found out we even had an ancestor on the Lewis and Clark expedition. I don't know who he was, but he wasn't Lewis or Clark. We went to school in Bozeman, and I lived in a town called Three Forks, which is the headwaters of the Missouri River, which branches off into the Madison and Beaver Head Rivers. I always used to have a mysterious sense of belonging in that part of the world, and not far from Three Forks was one of the campsites of Lewis and Clark. I spent several days up there sketching and scouting the area.

My first trip ever was with a company I used to work for in Denver and then in Montana, to a talcum powder producing company we had in Toulouse,

France. One of the world's largest talc mines was in the Pyrenees, but at that time the Pyrenees were still snow-shut so we couldn't see the mine sites. They hauled ore down in these big tran buckets in the on-season, and then put big stockpiles of talc ore at the mill site in France. We visited there and then went to Belgium and Brussels for part of that same trip.

In the last couple of years I was able to go with this company to Finland, Denmark, India, then back to Finland and Germany. I was doing environmental system audits in those places, and it was quite remarkable to see the cultures in these different places. You visit India after seeing it on TV, and it's that and then some. It's just remarkable. You don't appreciate the things we have in this country until you go to places like India and then come back home.

When I moved here, I wanted to get into the community and get to know people. I had gotten to know a few people by trying out for a part in the Hill Country Community Theater's Christmas play. I saw Rotary as a great way to be part of the community. I just missed being a charter member of the Daybreak Rotary Club in Marble Falls by about three months. I held a couple of offices and helped out with programs for a few years and then it came my turn to be president. I thought this was a heck of an opportunity to be part of this international organization. I didn't really understand until I became president how much it means worldwide. And you don't, I think, until you get involved in the district or at the president level. You start to see some of the programs that are done across the world and you see programs come back from there where really not much of our money is used. It's almost a shame that we don't donate much—so little goes such a long way. We put libraries together in south African countries and it is important to see how much that really means to them. It's pretty special.

We have a heck of an impact on kids around here with a program called RYLA (Rotary Youth Leadership Award). For the past five years we've sponsored two to three high school juniors, and our group is one of the fun groups that go to serve the kids breakfast. We head down there about 4:00 in the morning to make breakfast together. We started making breakfast tacos using different meats, but we thought this just wasn't cool enough. These kids appreciated this, so we started making road-kill breakfasts. We'd make armadillo road kill, roadrunner tacos, snake bits and bites. The kids would come in all blurry-eyed and we had labeled across the countertops what they could eat. They'd start laughing and really get into the spirit of things once they saw what we were doing. Road-kill café in the morning.

I think it is important to have a good time doing this and I think it means a lot. Some people are a real inspiration to Rotary. One member takes his donations to a particular group outside of Monterrey, Mexico. He takes that donation and several of his old buddies who are Rotarians and go up into the hills to visit some of the Old World Aztec tribes outside the hills of Monterrey, Mexico, in the same areas that Pancho Villa used to roam. They go up roads where you can't take vehicles. You have to strip down and take donkeys and pack your gear, whether it's wheelchairs, dental or medical beds, or other things up into the hills the hard way—by foot or donkey.

There's a book I wish I'd read while I was in high school, but I probably wasn't ready for it, and I wish all young people would read it, too. *Atlas Shrugged* by Ayn Rand. It's about how she grew up in one of those satellite Russian countries and watched her life be overrun by the communists and the consequences. She wrote her opus about the strength of the individual, and how you can be all that you can be, just apply yourself. Don't necessarily rely on the system or others to take care of you, because it leads to downfall in the end. It's not sustainable. I think her book is one of the greatest philosophical books written, next to the Bible. Everybody should read that, and I'd like to see more people appreciate those philosophies. I try to encourage my nephew who is old enough to hear those things to be a self-starter.

Recently I've run some marathons. I just finished my fourth one a couple days ago. I think the most powerful encouragement or lesson I could leave to somebody is simply to believe in yourself. I like a phrase somebody used recently: The human body has its limits, go out and find them. I would add that the human spirit and mind may have limits, go out and find them, see what they are, search and ask questions. Don't be satisfied with the status quo, be respectful of others, and live life.

Mihaela Hammond, Science Teacher
(formerly an ophthalmologist in Romania)

Marble Falls, Texas–Tulcea, Romania

Education is the key to all that you do in life.

Peggy Little

Marble Falls, Texas–Decatur, Illinois

I live in Burnet, Texas but I work in Marble Falls at a high school of choice. I was born in Decatur, Illinois. I spent a brief amount of time in Bloomington, Illinois, and five years in Logan Sport, Indiana before we settled in Cheyenne, Wyoming where I lived until I graduated from high school.

I lived in Lewis Fort, Indiana until I was about nine, in a very new subdivision on the outskirts of town. It was just my family and the next-door neighbors. I could tell you their names, their kids' names to this day. We played outside together and when one of the parents whistled we all ran. We rode our bikes and when the streetlights came on we all knew the routine. Our parents mowed the fields so we'd have a place to play baseball and football. It was very nice. We went to school during the week and to church on Sunday and cleaned the house on Saturday. It was a good routine and I had a wonderful, wonderful childhood.

The conditions at the time were slow-paced. The town I lived in was really an all-white town. I didn't realize what it was to live around African-Americans or Hispanics until I moved to Wyoming. Up until nine years old my whole world was a white world and I remember that being very influential in my life.

As a teenager, I lived in Cheyenne, Wyoming. At the time I didn't realize I was from a lower-income family. My father was an executive director of the YMCA and my mother was a stay-at-home mom. We were not affluent and we weren't poor.

I remember getting secondhand bicycles and stuff like that, but never thinking of that as being poor. That's the way life was. The conditions were important, especially as a teenager. I used to get $5.00 a week allowance—$2.50 to fill the gas tank and $2.50 for five lunches a week, and that was when I was in high school. I remember kids in high school saying they weren't going to smoke cigarettes when they got above thirty-five cents a pack.

We did the Friday night drive down the drag and back up to the alley to get a Coke and back down the drag and checking out your friends. And football games, town rivals, the two high schools, that was pretty big. Basketball was much bigger than football. But we just had fun, it was a good life, a teenage life, and teenagers don't change much. We had the in crowd; we had the jock crowd; we had the loners; we had those that just didn't fit in. I think that is the way you recognize kids, whether it was in the 1960s or 2012. We had skateboarders back then, and we have skateboarders now. It's interesting to watch teenagers want to show you how independent and different they are, and yet they all somehow fit into a group of kids doing the same thing.

Once I finished school I traveled. I couldn't get out of Cheyenne fast enough. I just wanted to see the world. I went to California and worked in Oakland for a while and lived in Martinez. Then I came back to Cheyenne where my parents and brothers were living. I got some odds-and-ends jobs, then I got my real estate license and sold real estate. I worked for Mountain Bell as a telephone operator, then moved on to the business office of Mountain Bell and worked there for a while. I worked for a lawyer for a very long time and earned my paralegal degree. I waited a lot of tables for a lot of different restaurants in Cheyenne.

I got married and then we moved to Houston. My husband had a job with a cable TV company that was booming in Houston at the time, so the children and I moved to Houston. I didn't have to work any longer—it was the first time I was ever a stay-at-home mom.

I got bored at home and thought I'd go to college, and I did. I got through college in three years with a degree in criminal justice from Southwest Texas State. I applied to teach criminal justice in high school. I received an emergency teacher's certification to do that. I thoroughly enjoyed teaching the high school kids. After my third year of teaching, I went back to school to receive my master's degree in school administration and became a principal.

After we had lived in Marble Falls for a while and got the kids through school, we bought some land and moved to the Austin area. I had been a principal at a school in Round Rock for a while and decided I really wanted to go to a school where I could make a difference and, hopefully, with kids in a small town. We selected Marble Falls because it is gorgeous and I love the water as well as the lakes around Marble Falls. Also, I like that it's a bedroom community of Austin. It's close enough to go to Austin if you want to and yet you still have that small-town flavor.

I've been in Marble Falls for ten years. I've been the principal and started out running the discipline facility only. My first year I had a dream, to start a school of choice with kids who did not fit in school or who had dropped out of school or who were in danger of dropping out—any of those scenarios. It would be a place for them to come and get their high school diplomas.

I was fortunate to initiate the concept and I opened the school. I have four full-time staff, two part-time, a secretary, and a student service coordinator. The highlight of the program has got to be graduation because graduation day is phenomenal. During our first year they told us we couldn't get twenty kids to come to a school like this in Marble Falls. Everybody would want to go to Marble Falls High School and nobody would want to do this. The first year we started out thinking we might get thirteen or fourteen to graduate, and this is going to be a good thing. We got real excited, and then we got real worried. We planned on graduation ceremony at a boys' and girls' club back in a little community room, and we ended up graduating thirty-eight kids.

We asked the kids if their parents were going to come and we got this response from the kids: Nobody's going to show up. They didn't know and we didn't know. We set up about 150 chairs and then we started getting worried. Man, this might look really bad but we'll have everybody sit at the front and it'll be okay. So graduation started and over four hundred people were there. We couldn't even get the graduates down an aisle to get up on a little tiny stage. It was amazing, and it has been overwhelming every year to see parents, grandparents, aunts, uncles, and the whole family see possibly the first graduate in the family. It made me realize this was my calling, this is where I need to be, and these are the kids who need me.

It was extremely emotional, and also the second year of graduation was very emotional for me. I always thought of writing a book called *Forty-two Roses*, because when the graduates walked across the stage—I did not know they were going to do this—every one handed me a rose. I had forty-two roses at the end of the night.

There were a lot of good tears, always joy. Seeing their light bulbs go on— they all of a sudden understand what they never understood before and now they can make sense of it. Or when I hear somebody say, "I am worth something, I can go on."

The criteria for students coming here is they have to be sixteen because, if possible, we like them to try to find a job. They can have work ethics as well. We like them to have at least eight credits because we are small and don't have a lot of electives for them to get everything they need to graduate with us. And a desire to have a high school diploma.

Ambassadors of the

Some people say these are at-risk students. That means a lot of things. Maybe they've already dropped out and could be at risk of not having a good career. It could be that they really messed up during their high school years and they are at risk of dropping out. It could be they are young girls and pregnant and they're at risk of maybe not having young adult lives to explore and learn without having babies to care for. There is a risk of losing a lot of things in their lives and we try to bring that back to them.

I think the students would say they like being treated as adults and having the opportunity to be able to go on in their lives. We give them the opportunity to see what's out there and encourage them to start reaching for goals. That's what they're really happy about here. They're being treated like adults and they like knowing what education is going to do for them because we really hammer them a lot.

Is there a 100 percent turnaround for these students? Not 100 percent on the first try, okay? We allow them to fail and it's okay to fail. What's not okay is not to get back up and try again. I have lots of kids here who want that high school diploma, they really do. But there's so much in their way. The number one reason is drugs. I can teach any kid, but I can't teach any kid on drugs. We get them help and we help them while we can, but tell them until you get clean and sober I can't get you to where you want to go. I don't feel like we fail, but we may go ahead and shoo them out the door. We had one kid who only needed two credits and it took him almost two years. This person was in and out, in and out, in and out. I said you got to go and he came back. He finally graduated and he's now working for Mercedes.

Selecting teachers was very interesting. I do not have a committee to select our teachers. I select them. All but one of my teachers started out as an elementary teacher. The reason for that is because I appreciate the nurturing and just the whole feel of elementary, and this is what the kids in this school need. They need to be not only taught academics, but to be shown how to be adults and how to be appreciative. Also, they need to know how to have manners and work ethics. These teachers are patient and they're kind and they don't get frustrated with kids very often. It takes a lot and they are very solid teachers, and I think it's because they had elementary teaching backgrounds.

We get some flack from other high school students who think our kids are just playing over here. I hear that a lot, especially my kids who have been sent from other schools in a disciplinary facility because they weren't behaving. My background, as I said, is in criminal justice, so I equate this a little bit to our justice system. People go to jail for a certain amount of time and they're going to come back out. Do you want them to come back out madder than they were when they went in, and more frustrated? Or would you like them to come out with some tools in their toolboxes, like how to behave the next time, how to make better choices and better decisions? So when kids come here because they can't make right choices I need to help them learn to make right choices. By doing that, I have to give them a hook. I can't just give them dry lectures. I need to hook them into something they can become a part of. Then it's theirs, they own it, they begin to listen, and then we project that onto the other aspects of their lives and how they can be more successful in theirs, too.

Some teachers at the high school resent me for doing what I am doing. How do I cope with this? I just try to be very friendly and very open. If I can be a part of the kids' lives while they're doing this and see students in a different light and not just in the classroom, I may be able to help them. To understand that education means a lot of things, not just academics, is significant in what we are trying to do to help these students survive in our world.

I have two brothers, an older one and a younger one. I laugh and tell people of all three of us, I'm the only one with a master's degree and I make one-fourth as much as either of my brothers makes. My mother lives with me, she's eighty-eight and has lung cancer. My mom's influence was clean, clean, clean. To this day I cannot get out of bed without making it. She was the epitome of the fifties housewife. The house was clean at all times, and dinner was on the table. She made me value that stay-at-home aspect and how much kids need that.

My father passed away when he was only fifty-eight and I was thirty. He had a profound impact on my life. He influenced me a great deal when he was the director of the YMCA. I grew up in a YMCA atmosphere and I grew up knowing I had to keep my body in good physical shape because it's the only body God gave me. Therefore, being physically fit helped me keep mentally fit as well. There were no couch potatoes in my house. We were always doing things all the time. I'll always remember my father's line, "Live your life with a Christian conscience and you'll be fine." Doesn't mean you have to be at church every Sunday.

My husband and I are not married right now. We got divorced a year ago, after twenty-seven years and I think it's just because of the lifestyle. We still are the best of friends. He worked most of our marriage, coming home only one weekend a month. It was very difficult after the kids were gone to have the same interests in the same things. But we live eight miles apart and he mows my yard and I clean his house. He worked for cable TV and he built cable TV systems all over the U.S. from Massachusetts to California. We ran our own cable TV company for quite a while and a construction company and did very good at it.

My children certainly are their mother's children. I have a daughter who lives in Missouri and she's finishing her last year in Colombia College with a double major, one in biology and one in chemistry. She's doing it on her own and raising four kids. My grandchildren are fourteen, nine, seven, and almost five. She's very good and wants to go into forensic science, so she'll do that. I have a daughter who lives in Round Rock and she's a special ed science teacher at McNeill High School. She has my grandson, Caleb, who will be nine next month. My other daughter, Ginger, lives right up the road in Leander and she has a son, Campton. She's the executive director of an association that brings people from other associations that do membership drives.

I would really like my children, grandchildren, and the young students I have served over the years to take time to *do* the little things they think about doing, but don't do. When you say, "I wish I'd sent a card," do it. I learned this when

Ambassadors of the

shopping and I saw a nice pair of shoes. I thought no, I'll get them later. I wish I'd gotten them later. Do it when it's in front of you. Do it, do it. Whatever you want to do, whether it's going on that camping trip, not worrying about your house being clean, saving money for that rainy day. I wish I'd bought it. I wish I'd gone then. If you think of somebody, pick up the phone and call them. Just do it.

I remember when my youngest one graduated from high school. I was kind of laughing and I said to her, well, you're the last one, everybody's graduated, so let's pack up the house go home. Kari Lee turned to me and said, "Mom we are home, we are. I wouldn't live anywhere but here, I am home."

Chris Patel, Hotel Owner

Marble Falls, Texas–Bilaspur, India

The United States is a great, great country. I am proud to be here with my wife and family. I love this country and I love the people.

Darren Queen

Marble Falls, Texas–Gillsville, Georgia

I was raised in Banks County, Georgia in the city of Gillsville. I came to Texas because the business we were engaged in required us to diversify our product and our product line fit very well into the petroleum industry in the oilfield. We moved here in 2007 and the economy was a little stronger here than in Georgia, but Georgia was still holding a good balance.

I had a very good general manager in Georgia and we discussed everything. If we were going to pioneer this new territory and product line, we all thought that I'd be more productive at it than hiring someone here. With the office in Georgia and one in Texas I knew I would be traveling back and forth a lot. So I flipped open a road atlas and I plotted near the center of Texas—I didn't want to fly out of a major city, I wanted to fly out of Austin or San Antonio. I placed my fingers around Marble Falls and New Braunfels and told my office manager to call the Chambers of Commerce and have them send some information. I was going to go over that information, then visit possibly three of those locations. That's how I picked Marble Falls.

The Chamber of Commerce here in Marble Falls sent the information we wanted immediately. Jeanne, in the visitor center, was relentless at sending me information. She gave me her personal cell phone number and agreed to meet us immediately when we came into town. She had interviews set up with the school board and it couldn't have worked better. That's one of the single most important reasons why I chose Marble Falls. Also, I knew if the Chamber was that interested in making sure we were welcomed that we would probably enjoy living in this town.

During my early years, I grew up in north Georgia on a poultry farm. The poultry industry is a large industry there. Within twenty miles of Gillsville, you have Gainesville and that's the poultry capital of the world. We had cattle and poultry until I was ten years old. From the time I was five or six I was able to help a little bit on the farm. I was always interested more in the cattle side than the poultry side. I had a very simple home life growing up in the country.

Teenage life was typical of that in any small town, living on a farm. We were up early in the morning, taking care of the poultry houses, and we helped with the cattle. We were real adamant churchgoers. That was what we lived for in a little town and almost everybody went to church. We went to church every morning, Sunday night, and Wednesday night. My father was very active at one of the local churches and so there weren't a lot of options on those things. That was kind of our hobby.

School was an adventure for me, and it was all right but I wasn't in the top of my class by any means. I was just a middle-of-the-road, average student. I completed high school and did what I had to, but I didn't go the extra mile most of the time. I just wanted to get the minimum and I thought I was wasting my time. I thought I needed to be working and making money.

I played a little sports, but no organized sports with the school. I played some Little League baseball and softball with some of the local church groups. School didn't get in my way, but from an early age, I was eager to work and get started on a career.

Before I graduated from high school, I was able to be exempt from my last-period class. I went to work for a company called Craven's Pottery in town. I'd come in every day at 3:00 and the owner allowed me to work as long as I wanted to at night. I poured concrete and I made concrete birdbaths that were ornamental pieces. He gave me a phenomenal opportunity because I could work long hours and I got paid for what I did. I learned how to manage my time, and later he let me hire people to work under me. So I had the opportunity to step into a management position at sixteen years of age. It was just phenomenal what my first boss brought to the table.

Right now I'm in the generator business. We still have a manufacturing and assembly operation in Georgia. I've been in Texas for three years and we just opened a sales and service office in Texas. The main thing we do is power operation equipment and we do backup equipment for county municipal buildings

Ambassadors of the

and hospitals, anyplace where they can't be without power. We design and install as well as build and service. Part of our business pertains to the oil industry. We build generators that run mobile equipment, whether it be an oil field rig or a water separation piece of equipment, or solids separation from water. Whatever would be in a remote location that needs power to run, we specialize in equipment that fits onto that type of equipment.

We're moving the corporate structure to Texas now, and the manufacturing and service will be in Georgia. We are interviewing salespeople now in Texas. I'm the owner of the company and we have ten employees. Hopefully within the next year we'll have three or four employees here in Texas, and then we'll see how it goes.

My family consists of my mother and father, an older brother, and an older sister. I'm the baby of the family. I have a son, Nolan, who is thirteen. I don't have any immediate family members involved in the company. I have one cousin who does sales for me. In the beginning when we were very small my wife, Michelle, used to help with the company and do some bookkeeping. But I try to keep the business separate from the family.

I said earlier that I coasted through school and now I am putting all my energy into what I do professionally, which is the opposite of what I did in high school. As I look back, I wasn't lazy. It was just that we were raised as hard workers and my parents were both very hard workers. I probably couldn't see any benefit to the classroom study at the time. To me it looked like an absolute waste of my time when I could be out there getting some stuff done.

In the last few years I've become an avid reader and I love to read books. Normally, I'll read a mix of about 60 percent business-related books and about 40 percent Christian books. I absolutely despised reading when I was in school. I didn't like math either. I almost quit over British literature. Caesar about put me out.

My inspiration to read today is because there's so much great information out there. As you go through the years as a businessperson you figure out where your shortcomings are. Things that were not important in my school years, like speech class, things I thought were crazy back then. Now, I try to fill those voids, gaining knowledge as fast as I can. And learning through books. It's a wonderful way to learn. Also, I am definitely a hands-on person.

I consider myself a pretty avid traveler, but not much international travel. I travel a lot through the U.S. and about seven to ten days a month I spend in Georgia. The rest time I spend in Texas or Louisiana, Oklahoma, and the surrounding territories. I'm still right in the middle of the business and I still do sales. I call all the customers, anyone west of Mississippi. We're getting to the point where it's a bit difficult, so I'm hoping to pull a bit of sales here because sales is my passion.

I've reached a lot of the milestones and goals I set for myself. I knew early on that I wanted to be an entrepreneur. In my early years I was always trying to head up everything. I didn't necessarily want to be in charge of everything, but I wanted to be a big part of everything that went on. Although I was successful with the first company, I didn't have problems with having authority over me. But I just loved the thought of doing something on my own where I had complete responsibility, that I had the ability for, and to see what I could accomplish. Do I consider myself an organizer? Yes, absolutely.

Everybody says the same thing to kids, and that is to really focus. The school years up until the twelfth grade are very, very important. If I was trying to go through the high points, these are the points I'd hit. Do as well as you can in kindergarten through twelfth grade, and I mean absolutely give it everything you've got. Read an enormous amount. I'm not an anti-sports guy, but I would balance my time well and try to get as much experience as possibly in the work industry or in the business field—don't lose sight of that. I think sometimes sports dominate children's time, so they don't get a hands-on experience and learn how to do things. I learned, at an early age, how to fix things like waterlines. Learn some real hands-on stuff and not just book knowledge. In everyday situations, it's okay to fall on your face because that's the best experience you can get. As a parent I stand back a lot and let my son make mistakes. I want him to make those mistakes because I want him to learn how to pick himself up from those situations.

Hard work, determination, and a very simple upbringing are important. It doesn't take a Harvard education to be successful in life and I'm not just defining success from a monetary standpoint. I'm a very happy person and I like what I do. I determine success when I wake up every morning and do what I do. I don't gauge it by the amount of money in the bank.

I'm very satisfied with Marble Falls and where we live. We are here as a family and that was important to us. That was a big deal when we moved the whole family because I could tell my son was completely against moving. You're talking about an eleven-year-old relocating a thousand miles away from his grandmother and that was not a happy day. Marble Falls, as a whole, and Faith Academy, I don't think anybody could have done more to welcome us. They made us feel at home anytime, without even being asked.

Traveling between Georgia and Texas, I get questions from people about both areas. From my standpoint, I tell them, it's kind of the same. In some parts of Texas the land looks the same as in Georgia. In Texas you have a mix of everything and you can go from desert to greenery. East Texas looks just like Georgia. One of the ways I describe Texas is it has a little bit of everything. You can go from the oilfields, to the coast, it doesn't matter what sector of business or what kind of region you want to live in, Texas has it somewhere.

I hope someone reading this story gets some inspiration out of it. Maybe this will give some confidence as a country, as a whole, not just the states of Texas or Georgia. I've had experiences from the East to the West and I believe in this great country.

Ambassadors of the

Samlee Namsombat, Cook

Marble Falls, Texas—Bangkok, Thailand

I want my children to be happy and successful.

MASON

Ambassadors of the

Gary Davel

Mason, Texas-Gweru, Zimbabwe

I was born in a town called Gweru in what was formerly Rhodesia and is now Zimbabwe. I grew up there until I came to America in June 1996. Anyone who knows anything about the history of Rhodesia would understand that during the time I was growing up, there was a terrorist war. When the government changed hands in 1993, black majority ruled. Things got very difficult for white people in Zimbabwe, so my wife, my son, and I and started trying to relocate. I had one son at that time. We had family in North America, and we wanted to be closer to family. Most of our family had lived in Zimbabwe and gone to other parts of the world, and we felt that it would be incumbent upon us to do the same. We felt that the Lord was leading us to the United States.

I grew up in rural Zimbabwe, or Rhodesia at that time, so much of the time was spent outdoors in the bush as we called it then—I don't know what they call the countryside here in America—in the tree house, hunting, or camping. That was very much the Rhodesian way of life.

When the opportunity arose to come to Mason, I visited for several weeks before the whole family moved here. There were a lot of similarities in the countryside, although Zimbabwe does have a much thicker bush as far as grass and so forth because the rainfall is much higher. But Mason has similarities with the Llano River and we have kayaking, which my sons love. There are several lakes nearby in the surrounding areas. Of course, there's hunting for my kids who are fifteen and nine—that is also a grand appeal.

We were tired in some ways of living in a city and we wanted to move to a smaller community where people know you and you know them. Those things are important, I think, to the very fabric of the culture of what we call America today. Mason has a climate of friendliness because it's not so big that you miss out on your neighbors. It's not so small that you're frustrated at your neighbors who are in your pocket. It's a nice size and the school district is a nice size, too.

There's a joke in Mason right now. People say, "Have you been to our town square recently? The traffic is so bad." I remember five years ago coming to Mason and if you had to wait at a stop sign behind two or three cars that was very unusual.

Fredericksburg is a beautiful place, but I think it has a different feeling and different things for people to do. It is a tourist mecca and I'm not sure we want to make Mason a tourist mecca as much as we want to have a very peaceful and quiet life.

I'm forty-six years old, believe it or not, and I look like I'm thirty-five, which is a good thing. I grew up in rural Rhodesia during a very difficult time because the terrorist war was taking up much of the political climate and the emotional climate. There was so much going on in the country at that time and my family life was very sheltered. Growing up in rural Rhodesia was much like living in America in the '60s and '50s, after WWII. Life was very sheltered and family-oriented. Television was just beginning to be thought about. Movies and Hollywood were not things that had proliferated in our society as much as today.

My upbringing, by and large, was difficult and we were not wealthy by any means. But we had everything that we needed. We lived on a ten-acre plot outside of the city I was born in. We had a few dairy cows and an orchard. We had enough space for my brother and me to run ruckus and enjoy outside life. The climate in Zimbabwe was very conducive to being outside. Life was generally good.

Teenage life got a little harder, of course, and the terrorist war was still going on at that time and I was concerned about being drafted into the military. So my parents shipped me off to South Africa to go to school for two years. It was a very, very difficult time in my life, being away from family. I did have some wonderful aspects of my life, too. I spent a lot of time with my father outside because he was an engineer. He had a workshop and all the gizmos that one would expect from an engineer. I could weld by the time I was twelve. I could

Ambassadors of the

build and I could do things that the average child couldn't. I grew up with a mechanical background.

My mother is still alive and lives in New Zealand. My parents had a difficult relationship and there was a lot of tension in the home. They were not Christians. There was a lot of misunderstanding and unresolved conflict—there was no such thing in our house as conflict resolution.

School was great. I was a great student and I loved school. I was very conscientious. I think I could've gone much further in life, in terms of accomplishing a lot more, had I had the emotional stability I needed but didn't get at home. I loved sports, played rugby, played cricket. I was a champion swimmer in high school and I loved it. I played a game equivalent to racquetball and I enjoyed that and I also played water polo. I was a very sporting individual. Generally, outside of the house I had a great existence.

After high school it was a bit of a difficult transition because my father died in 1983, which was my graduating year. I really didn't know what I wanted to do with my life, but that was the catalyst for me coming to know the Lord. My father passed away on April 18, it was actually Zimbabwe's Independence Day. Not long after that, I came to know Jesus Christ as my personal Lord and Savior. So my father's death was a catalyst for God to touch my life in a very unusual way, in a way that I never dreamed or even thought.

From that moment my life took on a different journey. I began to see life through different eyes. I started to go into the electrical field because I wanted to become an electrician. In those days in Zimbabwe they had what is called an apprenticeship. You would go sign up for a four-year apprenticeship and learn the trade. Because my father had been an engineer I thought that would be something I'd like to do. But I didn't realize that I had undeveloped skills, for example, in writing and literature. I did a year of electrical apprenticeship.

At that time, 1985, things were declining severely in the country. I intended to leave Zimbabwe and go to South Africa, so I resigned in the electrical field with intentions to go to South Africa, but I never went. I worked briefly for a company called Farm-Aid cash supplies. It was much like a town and country building supply shop. Next I went to work for the largest manufacturing company in southern Africa.

The most important factor that led me into my ministry, as I reflect back now with all my education and what I've accomplished, is I wanted to see people's lives and families healthy. A lot of other things precipitated my desire to go into ministry. My primary focus and purpose really is to please Him. But secondly, I have this innate desire to help people get better, emotionally and mentally, because I didn't receive a lot of help in my life.

I've been in full-time ministry for fifteen years. Before Mason I was in Euless, Texas and then, of course, before that back in Zimbabwe at Emmanuel Fellowship in the town where I grew up.

We have a one-year-old baby, so that keeps us very busy. I have a son who will be fifteen in November and a nine-year-old. We love to kayak and we enjoy going fishing. I recently learned to fly fish and I really love it. I also play an acoustic guitar and the keyboard.

My wife is from a farming community in Africa, and we married before we came to the States. None of her family is in Zimbabwe. Both of our families are scattered around the world. I talk to my mother every chance I have. She lives in New Zealand and our relationship is a healthy one.

The River of Life Church is the fourth church that I've been involved in, ever, in my whole entire life. It has probably been the best as far as people go. Mason is like one big family in a lot of ways. Then you take it down to a smaller level of the church and people become even more of a family. People here are very kind and friendly. You have the odd one that is just ornery. But by and large, people genuinely care. Christians care and they care for the church, especially. They are caring of me, caring of my family, caring of one another. We are one big family and we have a desire to grow in the Lord. I've never pastored a church like this before. The people are open. They desire more spiritual things, they're hungry for spiritual things, they want to learn. Of course, me being from Zimbabwe and having this accent, I guess makes me something of an anomaly.

I'm very busy in Mason because people have needs. A lot of those needs are based on assumptions, wrong assumptions, wrong beliefs. That's where I come in. I try to help people redirect their focus on the Lord and put those needs in the proper place. I spend a lot of time helping people, talking to people, sometimes counseling marriages, sometimes helping with families.

Sometimes a rancher will come by and pick me up in his truck and there we go. I'm not bound to the office—it's very flexible in a lot of ways. It's a large church, over 200 people. I'm the only one on pastoral staff that is here full time. Discipleship is a big thing to me. I believe that people need to be discipled and the best way to do that is one-and-one and in small groups. We spend a lot of time developing discipleship and adult Bible study. Things that can help people grow spiritually and that takes time. My life is people.

I wasn't always a people-oriented person. Coming out of a somewhat dysfunctional family, I was not equipped to help people. I was a very austere individual. I was the kind of guy that if you crossed me I'd put you on my black list. But a lot of that was just hurt and pain. And hurt people hurt people. That is all gone now and my desire is to help people and help them to grow.

Recently, I went to Nigeria with my son and a gentleman from church. The abject poverty! Nigeria is another country with a lot of anomalies. It is deeply entrenched in corruption, as is Zimbabwe today. I don't think I'd try to relate to people in general as much as I'd try to touch the ones and twos that can understand. One thing I've realized in life is that to have lofty goals can sometimes bring anxiety into your life. Those who can understand are the ones I focus on and those are the people who have the keen interest that I feel I need to know. I'm not too concerned about the average American because the average American is very focused. I know some people who've never left Texas and there are some people who maybe have not left Mason. I don't worry about that. I find the ones and twos—Jesus only had twelve and I can't expect more than that.

Ambassadors of the

We live life from the knowledge we know, from the knowledge we have, and so knowledge changes. People change.

I would like people to know me as a man of honor. I want people to remember me as a person who really honored God, who really loved God, and really worshiped God. My heart and soul belonged to the Lord, and even if I was in a secular job, even if I was doing engineering or something else, I would still want that. I don't say that because I'm a pastor, I say that because when I got saved at nineteen I was ready to be saved. My life was devoted to the Lord even before I went full time into the ministry because I loved the Lord. And as a worshiper, worship leader, I want people to remember me as a man who really worshiped God like King David. He was a man after God's own heart.

I want people to realize freedom, real freedom, true freedom. We live in a country that espouses freedom. We are bathed in independence, but I want people to realize that true freedom only comes when we worship God. True freedom only comes when we honor God. America can only be free when we honor God and nothing else is going to provide us that freedom. In the end we honor God, and we bless Him for what he has done for us and for what he's going to do. All the political badgering is not going to help.

I love this country. I deeply love this country, and I think I love America more sometimes than the average American. I know what it is like to lose a country and I know what it's like to leave a culture that was eclipsed. I know what it's like to come to another country and watch all the telltale signs of a culture that is moving into eclipse. I think God brought me to America to help Americans in a lot of ways to work through that, help them to see that, help them to understand that, help them grieve over that. That's what people are doing.

Scott Haupert

Mason, Texas–Des Moines, Iowa

I was born in 1967 in a small community called Streeter, which is about twelve miles from the center of Des Moines, Iowa. Des Moines is the capital city of Iowa and I lived in a suburban-type old neighborhood not far from downtown. Although people think Iowa is the corn belt with farms everywhere, it was a city experience, an urban experience even though it was in Iowa. I'd say I had a pretty much ideal upbringing with a sister and both parents. My parents have been married for over fifty years. I had a middle-class to upper-middle-class upbringing, so we had what we needed.

I went to public school in Iowa, and at the time I was growing up, Iowa always ranked number one in the educational system out of all fifty states, so my education was awesome. I went to elementary school, junior high school, and then high school. I was a good student with As and Bs, but I just did what I had to do to get by. I could've probably produced better grades had I worked to my

Ambassadors of the

potential, but I liked certain subjects better than others. I'm a creative person so the arts, reading, the English language, and music were my things. I played violin and viola. I did not excel in biology, chemistry, or history—they didn't interest me at all.

After high school I had my first introduction to Texas, where I went to college. I applied to the University of Iowa and to Luther College, a really awesome private school in Decorah, Iowa. My third choice—and it was a choice I wanted—was Trinity University in San Antonio. I opted to go to Trinity. I majored in journalism with a minor in music. I graduated after four years from Trinity and went to Yale and received a master's degree in music.

After I completed my master's I moved to Los Angles. I was a professional musician for a number of years. I was in the San Diego Symphony and also in the Los Angeles Opera orchestra. But I made most of my living doing studio work, records and jingles. I did over 300 motion pictures scores, including *The Titanic*, *Jurassic Park*, and *Forrest Gump*, which were all big-budgeted musically.

I continued in my musical career but it was kind of in phases. I wanted to move back to Texas because the thrill of being in California was waning. I came back here in '94, checked out Austin, and ended up moving here. I kept an apartment in Austin for the next six years and flew back and forth to California every week or two to do sessions. I went from San Antonio to Austin, one or the other, back and forth, and kept an apartment as well as a car there.

When I was at Trinity I had a partner, Manny, and we've been together for twenty-two years. He went to Connecticut with me. He was at St. Mary's and then we went to LA together. After the floods and the riots and being smack in the middle of the Rodney King situation and smack in the middle of North Ridge earthquake where freeway overpasses around the neighborhood we lived collapsed—I mean it was pretty awful—I wanted to go back home. And Mason feels like home.

Home is Texas, not Iowa, not Connecticut, not New England, not southern California. I preferred Texas and that's where I wanted to plant myself. I don't know if I'd want to live anywhere in Texas but the Hill Country because it is just a magical place. I like the people, the culture, the landscape, the food, and the weather is agreeable to me.

Manny's parents are from Mason and he grew up here. We tried Austin and sublet an apartment for five months. We kept coming out here to visit his family and you just get this kind of relaxed feeling when you cross the county line. It felt so comfortable. It's a very attractive, quaint town and I felt momentum coming this direction from places like Fredericksburg that are exploding with opportunities and tourism. Here in Mason, at that time, it was almost like a ghost town. There were a lot of empty buildings on the square and ridiculously inexpensive property at that time. We bought some properties thinking that good things would happen here and it might be fun to create a job for ourselves by starting one business. Now it's three.

My music is on the back burner. I'm kind of on sabbatical and I'm okay with that. I get an itch every now and then. I could always find opportunities to play.

I gave a few recitals here in town so people got to know me and hear me play. But I got burned out a little bit and I was doing it just for the money at the end. It wasn't very fulfilling. I'm not the type to do something and keep doing something for the rest of my life if I am not engaged in it and fulfilled.

We bought an old dilapidated Texaco gas station on the corner square. It's called Santos and we completely restored and remodeled it and converted it from a gas station to a restaurant. Manny's mother is an incredible, intuitive, and amazing cook and already had a reputation around town for being one mean cook. We roped her into the whole deal and started Santo's in 1998. It quickly became successful enough to receive a lot of great press and people came from far away just to eat there. So it was a great experience.

We also have a winery. We kind of walked into that. We bought the little building next to the restaurant that went for sale so there'd be no issues with parking if someone else bought it. When the tenants moved out and it was empty, we decided to do something different.

Our neighbor across the creek was the first guy to plant a vineyard here and we became good friends. One thing led to another and we decided to team up and open a small boutique winery and make wine. Right as the law changed in Texas to allow wineries to exist in counties that are dry—a constitutional amendment passed in 2003. The idea behind it was to encourage the growth of the wine industry and agritourism, so the law opened the door for us to do that. We had to go through some difficult public hearings to get a permit to have a winery in that location, but we persevered and now the Sandstone Winery is seven years old.

It's doing great. It's a winery and it's also part gallery. We teamed up with a world-famous artist who lives here named Bill Worrell. His art was inspired by pictographs on the lower Pecos. He's right on the plaza in Santa Fe and he's in galleries all over the Southwest, including Sedona and Taos. He agreed to do the artwork for our wine label so we teamed up with him and started selling his art also. Part of the gallery has paintings and bronzes by this particular artist. So it's basically food, wine, art, and now there's the wine bar where we added music a couple times of month, and we'll have light music here.

This area is more tourist-driven than anything. But there's a great local following. We're on the edge of the Hill Country so that's the only drawback about having a business here—it's just not terribly convenient to get to from anywhere. If you think of the triangle, we are exactly equidistant to three major cities: San Angelo, Austin, and San Antonio, all exactly 100 miles away. We get traffic from there—a major highway goes through here, so a lot of people from Lubbock, Abilene, or San Angelo who are going to San Antonio or Austin pass through here. It's kind of a way station for a lot of people and they'll stop, eat lunch, and taste wine. The Texas Department of Agriculture spends a lot of money promoting the wine industry so it's tourist-driven and people get out and try it out.

Neither Manny nor I had any experience or background in the wine industry, other than enjoying wine in the past, but we didn't really know anything about it. We learned on the job. We made seven vintages of wine with our winemaker,

Ambassadors of the

our great neighbor. He's the wine mixer and he went to Harvard. He was an interesting guy with an interesting story, too, but he was born in Texas. We saw other Texas wines and developed a palette by sampling all different styles, types of wines.

My hobbies and interests are simple, but I have fun. I am a news junkie. I love news and current events. Music is also an important part of my life. I exercise every day, jog, walk, and bike. I have quite a menagerie of animals. We have gazillions of animals out at the ranch, including longhorns, lots of cats and dogs, geese, a peacock, goats, and chickens. We breed longhorns and have chickens for eggs. We also have three horses. It takes time and energy to take care of that but we do it for the love of it.

My parents are in their seventies and they come down here two or three times a year and stay for about three weeks. They still live in Des Moines. My dad was one of the editors of *Better Homes and Gardens* magazine, which is based in Des Moines. My mother is an artist and made her living as a graphic designer and art director for the same company, designing cookbooks and magazines in Des Moines. I have a sister, who still lives in Des Moines, married with three kids and is a full-time freelance graphic designer. She is very, very busy and very successful, working out of her home for major corporations all over, everywhere. Although I seem to take after my mother, there's a lot of creativity in the family.

Don't laugh, I'm actually a smidgen Native American, from Pocahontas and John Smith. It's in books, it's traced back, I'm in the books, I'm whatever kind of Indian she was. It's very diluted but I know because I have been asked many times about it.

If the young people of today were to observe me and look at me as an example, I would hope they'd see me treating everyone with kindness, treating everyone with an equal amount of respect. I'd say try to have everything you do be a win-win situation and leave it better that you found it. There are all kinds of ways I could describe it, like making things beautiful, like taking things that are rundown and dilapidated and bringing them back to life in an attractive way—that may even become contagious to other people. Good things happen from creativity and there are positive ways to make the world a better place and a nicer experience. Take care of the people around you that you love and give as well as receive grace.

Monica Hinckley

Mason, Texas–Guayaquil, Ecuador

My real name is Monica Maria Theresa Veronica Vastedas Valenzuela de Hinckley. I am originally from Guayaquil, Ecuador, South America. I am number three of six children, five girls with the last one a boy, from a Catholic family. Both parents came from Ecuador and we immigrated to the U.S. when I was two years old. I feel I am as American as anybody else. My father needed some help and my parents wanted a son to help them. I was very much a tomboy growing up and I can remember helping my father all the time. He was petroleum engineer and he was home only on weekends. He had to go where the oil wells were and I was not allowed to go, because girls back then could not do anything like that.

He built hand radios and I helped him with the little transistors as well as repairs on the car. I came here when I was two and we lived in Houston. We lived in the U.S. for school and in summers we went back to Ecuador and lived with my grandmother, my mother's family in Guayaquil. My father's family was

Ambassadors of the

from Quito, Ecuador, which is the capital city. It was cold in Quito whereas Guayaquil was warm because it's a port city, very much like Houston as far as weather and range of people.

I grew up in both cultures. My home life was very much Spanish but my parents insisted we speak perfect English, with no accent. I've even been accused here in Mason of having a New York accent. I went to a private girls' school called Duchesne Academy of the Sacred Heart for fifth and sixth grades. That was the most wonderful memory, the peak moment of my youth.

My parents were from what I would call the elite or high-class families in Ecuador. There were ten families in the "ruling class" and it's difficult to talk about this because people nowadays do not understand. We were landed gentry. We had servants, we had properties, land, farms, houses, and vacation homes. My relatives down there still have some of that, not quite as much. There was never a middle class when I was growing up.

My mother was Angela Barriga Valenzuela, and she grew up in Europe—she was taken to Europe when she was only three months old. Her education was primarily French, and her second language was English while she was in boarding school. She went back to Ecuador when she was twelve, when the war broke out. Now she had to speak Spanish. She was trilingual. For her Europe was the "mother country" even though she was from Ecuador.

My father's heritage was Basque and he also came from a high-class and very good quality family. He is typical Basque, short, squatty body, big chest, good lungs, and very warlike. He could sure turn on his temper when he wanted to. My mother was also very quick-tempered—maybe that's normal in Latin women.

My parents were raised with nannies or nurses. One of my mother's dreams was to have direct involvement with her children. She resented the fact that she was presented to her mother everyday at 5:00. She loved her mother, but had very little emotional contact with her.

I became a naturalized citizen of the United States in 1964 when I was eleven. We all had to go through the test and raise our right hands. My dad became a citizen at the same time as all the kids. I remember going to court and doing fingerprints. I tell people that I am more American, more Texan, than any of you because you all were just born here. I chose to come here. I changed citizenship, which is a really big deal when you consider that my family heritage was in Ecuador.

My teenage years were more difficult. In fact, I would say I was miserable. But I think that's part of being a teenager. You have both the identity crisis thing going on and you want to fit in. I didn't fit into either the U.S. or Ecuador.

I graduated from eighth grade from my parochial school and went to Memorial High School, which was a big high school in Houston. I was fifteen and in ninth grade and I was clueless, totally clueless. They were doing the rah-rah football thing and I had absolutely no clue and no home life that would give me any insight into what was going on. We were in a different place and level. My parents were involved in a group called the International Studies. They sponsored people from other countries. My father was a conciliator for Ecuador from the U.S. We had a lot of international visitors, which for our neighborhood and our society was very rare. I could see that I was in another world compared to the kids in high school.

When I was a junior and beginning to fit in, the unexpected happened. We moved back to Ecuador. My two older sisters were in college. I went with them and oh my gosh, talk about another different world. I didn't fit in with what they were doing and I didn't have a clue about anything. Soccer was a big thing and I don't think I'd ever seen a soccer ball at that point. I'm now an awkward seventeen-year-old beginning to develop and such. I was in the American School in Guayaquil and it had two parts. One side was American ex-patriots, mainly kids of missionaries in South America. I was surrounded by that Catholic environment. I was introduced to the Bible, which in the old Catholic Church before Vatican II, the common person did not have access to or was not encouraged to read the Bible.

The saddest point in my life was high school graduation. There were five kids in the American school portion and I was fifth in my class. The school year schedule in Ecuador was opposite the way it was in the U.S. It was the end of the year, in May, when we moved back and we graduated in January. That was my senior year. It was a lousy mess. Up until that point I'd been making good grades. I was a very diligent child and I was heading towards engineering, greatly influenced by my father.

Another thing I enjoyed here in the U.S. were the drafting classes. I loved drawing and art. I was a very creative person and I liked to make things. I graduated from high school when I was only seventeen—I was always the youngest in my class. I stayed in Ecuador for a year after I graduated. My mother let me audit classes at the University in Ecuador. In Guayaquil, there's a university called the University Catolica (Catholic University). It's run by the church but it's not church-oriented. I audited classes in architecture but I didn't have enough Spanish language skills because I went to school in the U.S.

My dream was to come back to the U.S. and go to school at A&M. I wanted to be an engineer. My parents allowed me to do it. I had no clue at that time that A&M was all male. Fortunately, the year that I signed up as an eighteen-year-old they allowed women on campus. They had built a dorm, which was a marvel of an engineer feat, a two-tower structure, and filled one side with women and the other side with men.

I did very well at A&M once I realized what was going on and I was more sure of myself. I was the only girl in engineering in my class. I was maybe one of eight girls in the whole bit. I had a great time and I met my husband there. We both received our degrees in 1976, but we were married in 1975. I chased after him and I got what I wanted. I graduated in engineering technology, which was supposed to be a lot of drawing and a lot of drafting. Brent, my husband, received his degree in pre-architecture, it's called environmental design. My first job was part-time while in school and he was a janitor at the Methodist church where we were married. I was working at an impeller factory that makes aluminum blades for silos. I had gone through classes of foundry and miracle control machinery and I was very mechanically inclined. I worked at the factory and drew the plans for the blades. I enjoyed that.

We came to Dallas because he wanted to go to seminary to be a Methodist preacher. In the meantime he worked in picture framing. He was good at it and got a pretty good salary. I became an electrical design engineer and was there for many years. We lived in Dallas for twelve years and my husband bought and owned a picture frame shop. I was still working as an engineer and making good money. We could afford to move and we did. His mother grew up in Art, Texas just outside of Mason.

We came here every summer or whenever we had vacation time to visit Grandma on her 800-acre ranch, which was a beautiful, big, wide-open space. The children loved it. On the way home we'd all be crying, because we loved the place. We came here with the idea that we'll stay here one year. If I couldn't find work or if the children, who were nine and eleven, found it difficult we could go back to the city. I'd never lived in a rural environment—I lived in the city all the time.

The first two years, I commuted every so often because I had jobs from the companies I was still working for in Dallas. Back then we didn't have computers, so we'd put papers on a seat on the bus and send them off. Finally, I decided it was too far and Austin and San Antonio were only two hours away. I went to Austin, found a job, and worked until 2002 when I was laid off. My last job was at Motorola as a facilities engineer. We had thirty-five buildings and I was made power engineer. I did locating switches, lights, and remodeling, and I loved my work. I commuted Monday through Thursdays, so Brent was at home with the kids. On the weekends I was wife and mother and during the week I was an engineer.

My husband and I have five businesses in Mason. We have the Red Door Bed and Breakfast and the Country Store, the variety store downstairs. We have the Lone Star Laundry that we built two years ago because the town didn't have any laundry facilities. We have a property account and three buildings that are leased. We just closed one, an antique mall where you rent booth space. I'm the "maintenance man" for all of it and it's a job! My husband is the mayor of Mason. Being mayor was an additional task he took on after organizing the businesses. He hoped he could help improve the community for everyone. We started the businesses and he developed and expanded them in the years that I was working. All the money I made went into the businesses and we were very frugal.

I've come from a long way and I am very happy to be here. I try to tell people about my history but it's so different, so unique from their experiences that I don't think I'm reaching them. There's good and there's bad in every life experience, but we have to connect and bring the good things through.

One of the things I see in today's society, and I think we all see it, is a degradation of morals, courtesy, and respect. They weren't taught to me, they were born in me. That's something I need to pass on to my children and grandchildren. I hope they have already learned these important traits. I'm very proud of my grandchildren and of my daughter-in-law, especially since I never had a girl, just my two boys. My daughter-in-law is from Fredericksburg and they live now in Fredericksburg. She is a sweetheart and she is home-schooling their children. They were missionaries in Central America for five years; the oldest child was born in Honduras. From the beginning my son was going to be a priest and my daughter-in-law was going to be a nun. We convinced them when they were in college they needed to be a good Catholic family and I am very glad we did. I have one final comment. We will never have peace on this earth until everybody shakes hands with one another.

MEDINA

Tanya Authement

Medina, Texas–Nikolaev, Ukraine

In Russia you have a full name and a short name. Tatiana is my official name and Tanya is my short name. I was born in the former Soviet Union. Now the town I was born in, Nikolaev, is in the Ukraine. When I was about four years old, we moved to the town of Serov in the Ural Mountains. My parents were producers in the theater. It was very big back then in the former Soviet Union. We lived in an apartment. These were typical buildings, which all looked alike. The town had a lot of snow every winter and winters were long.

I went to the first grade there but I don't remember anything about it. After the first grade my father was offered a promotion in a new theater in Tiraspol in what is now Moldova. Back then it was the Moldavian Soviet Socialist Republic. It was a small republic; the town was about 250,000 people. This is where I grew up and graduated from high school.

The government gave us an apartment on the fourth story of a five-story building, with no elevator, but the climate was a lot better. There was no snow but lots of tomatoes and roses. I grew up eating lots of grapes. It was really was a wonderful time.

I went to a specialized school, Number Six—that's how Russian schools are called, we don't give them names, just numbers. We had English language, English Literature, history in English, geography in English, and everything you can think of except math and science in English starting from the fourth grade. So my English was quite good except my knowledge of history in English was zero. I didn't have enough vocabulary yet. We had a pretty tough school but very good teachers. I really enjoyed going to school because it only had sixteen kids in the graduating class. I think all the kids in high school did also. At least 90 percent went on to college after graduation.

I played basketball for the Republic, the small Republic of Moldova. I'm not very tall but I was very quick. We were called Young Pioneers, which was similar to the Girl Scouts and Boy Scouts. We always did things together like going to the disco and dancing. My main friends were the girls I played with. We also did a lot of theater. I was in the theater and my mother was the lead actress at the theater. I don't know the exact English for it but my father was head of the theater and an actor in the movies.

In school I was good at chemistry, thanks to a very good teacher. I was quite good with math but I wanted to do something with chemistry and my mother persuaded me not to do that. I held first place in the Republic in chemistry because Russians are very big on all these championships and I was number one in English language among specialized schools. So I decided to do something with languages and math. I chose international business because I wanted to get out of the country, I wanted to travel. Russians could not leave the country unless we were diplomats or worked for an embassy. We didn't have, back then, the freedom to just buy a ticket and go someplace.

I chose the only existing college in the former Soviet Union, which was in Moscow. It was and still is part of the Moscow State University, but it is a diplomatic college and it's called the Institute of Asian and African Studies. My parents were very supportive of me and they wanted me to go there. They were hoping I would get in because it was pretty much impossible for a girl not from Moscow, not being a Communist Party member, not having any connections or relatives in Moscow. I did get in. I still don't know how, but I did. Only fifty kids were accepted to the first year of university—none of them girls, except me. None of them were Jewish. None. All of them were either Communist Party members, which I never was, or they were very good academically, which I was. Jewish people were discriminated against, though not officially. Certain institutes would not take a Jewish person if it said on your passport. This passport would give your nationality and Jewish in Russia is a nationality. I am Russian.

Although I received a diploma in international business relations it was a very difficult to get a job. For a while I couldn't do anything with it because I was not a Moscow citizen. I had to stay in Moscow because this is where all the embassies were as well as all the foreigners, and my major was Chinese language. There was nowhere else to go. However, I didn't have the so-called stamp in my passport saying that you live at this and that street. You could not just rent an apartment or a house back in the seventies, so you either had to marry a Muscovite or do something else. So I was there, graduated first in my class with a 4.0 GPA and I couldn't get a job. I didn't get a job for three years.

I attributed it to what is called "The System." It's not political, it's just the system of controlling people, I guess. We had our passports issued to us when we were sixteen. You have to have a stamp in your passport to prove you are a Muscovite. Well, I was not. I was from Tiraspol because this is where my family lived. I was just living in a dormitory and going to college. If you have a regular career you can be an engineer anywhere. But with my diploma I could be a diplomat only in Moscow. But I couldn't be a diplomat because I was not a Muscovite. It was a vicious circle and it was broken only when I married a young Russian man who was a Muscovite. That's when it changed for me and I could get a job.

I taught Chinese in different ministries and became a professor at the institute where I worked. I was the head of the Department of Chinese Language for students who wanted to pursue engineering careers and I started that as well as the curriculum. I continued teaching at different levels and I taught Chinese and English to businessmen who wanted to travel abroad; their countries would send them because the country was opening at that time. I also taught middle school, which was a specialized school for kids whose parents went overseas but couldn't take the kids. For some reason they would wait in Moscow and go to a specialized Chinese school.

I loved teaching. I just like to see the kids at the beginning because they are fascinated, and then they're upset if they're told they cannot join the group because not everybody can study Chinese because it's very hard. There is a selection process. The first year of learning Chinese is difficult. But Chinese is not difficult if you learn the system, which is the key. I do have a good ear for languages. We had very good times.

My Russian husband, whom I met at the same institute, was a diplomat/translator as I was. He became a translator in the Army because at that point we were helping our Afghan friends to make their revolution in 1979. He was on the battlefield and a lot of our friends actually died. But he survived and he was an interpreter for the general. He was very good with languages. We were on the same faculty and he majored in international business relations as well but he had Farsi language or Pashto, which are Afghan-Iranian languages.

Several books were written about my parents because they were the first dissidents in the Russian Gulag. They met in the Gulag. My mother was there for

Ambassadors of the

fifteen years. She was put there at eighteen years of age because she was married to a German. The Red Army marched into Germany and collected everybody they thought belonged back home and put them in prison. Some were killed. My mother survived. My father was a political dissident and he was not supposed to be liberated but Stalin died in 1953. My parents were released in 1955 and they were issued a document with apologies. I was born in 1956. Now, they both have died.

My parents never told me about their lives in the Russian Gulag. They were so much afraid, even though they were released people. People never talked about it. They did not want to jeopardize my future. That's why they never thought I'd be able to get into the institute I got into, but I didn't know anything about it. They told me when I was about twenty-four and I was in shock. But I was old enough to understand what really happened because my mother returned to Germany and she became a prominent citizen and was very active in the Catholic church as well as the community. She was well respected there so I knew a lot about her life and why and how. It was fascinating but very tragic.

My father died in Tiraspol when I was in China. He died of heart failure. They couldn't save him because doctors in Russia, in little towns at that time, were not prepared for emergencies, so if something God forbid happened they were held responsible. On a lot of occasions people died.

Before I went to the United States I went to China because I was a professor in Moscow University and I was the only one who actually was teaching Chinese successfully. I'd never been to China because back then you had to be a Communist Party leader or just a Communist Party member and I was not. I refused to be. For no particular reason, I just didn't want to.

Finally my turn came in 1989. I went there to pursue my Chinese career, in the real world. I went to Guangzhou to Sun Yat-Sen Zhongshan University. It's in Canton right across from Hong Kong. Then I went to Beijing and I met my husband there, who happened to be an American. I married him in Beijing. It's a very interesting story because it was the first marriage after the Cold War between a Russian and an American in China. My embassy, the Soviet Union, refused to marry us and they said, "If you go and Americans marry you, we will not arrest you." Well, the Americans refused to marry us, and they said, "Well, if Soviets don't want to marry you guys, we don't have to." It was so funny. I spoke Chinese very well, so we married in a Chinese marriage office. Both countries accepted.

My first husband is alive back in Russia and is married for the second time I think. We have a daughter together and I don't believe he has any more children. I took my daughter with me.

That is a true story about the Russians and the Americans refusing to marry us. The Chinese married us but they made us take tests, because in China you have to be healthy when you get married. It's funny but they check your health. You also have to say that you'll have just one child. There are certain rules and they wanted me to follow the rules. I told them if my future husband has a disease that you find, do you think I'm not going to marry him? I still will! So it was a bit of a fight, but we got married. My husband was working cooking Italian food in a Holiday Inn and in China. It's a big chain and it's very luxurious. Hotels in China are quite luxurious. That was in 1990. I was in China about three years.

Next we went to Egypt where I taught English, but mainly because my husband got a job there. We lived in Egypt for a bit more than a year. After that, we decided it was time to return to the United States for no particular reason, just decided it was a good time. That was 1993. I'd never been to the United States so I figured, okay, let's try.

My husband was from the Bronx. We went to New York City but it didn't work out the way it could have. We moved to Houston because my husband—who is my ex-husband now—was looking for a job in Texas and he had some difficulties. We got a divorce in 1995.

I worked for a long time at the Exxon Development Company in Houston. It was a big thing when the oil project started in Russia. I was the interpreter/translator/advisor to several presidents of this company in the Russian division. I stayed there for ten-plus years and built a very good career and I loved it.

During that time, I met Matt Authement, married him, and we've been together for fifteen years. He lived in Houston and we met at a business meeting when diplomats from Siberia came over to solicit business from oil companies so that oil companies could go to Siberia. I was an interpreter at the meeting and my husband was in the audience representing one company. We met, dated, and we married in 1997.

He was offered a job overseas, on Sakhalin Island, which is a skinny island north of Japan. He went there for about a year. In the meantime, the manager on my job, who had great family values, offered me a job on Sakhalin Island with the Exxon Company. So, I joined my husband there and we lived on Sakhalin Island for about three years. I had two daughters. One was a student at UT in Austin and my little one, Mary, was with us on the island. She had to go to a Russian school because international schools were not available. Her Russian skills were not good enough and we had to put her into a boarding school in Japan while we were overseas. We returned when she was in ninth grade.

My husband bought a ranch and we decided to raise cows. My husband loves Texas and we traveled a lot in the Hill Country because I think it's the most beautiful part of Texas and I really love it here. We traveled a lot, camped out, and we spent all our free time here in the Hill Country. My husband started looking on the Internet while he was overseas and he decided to buy this ranch. We built this little house, fenced everything, dammed the river, and on and on. We just moved in. Our daughter goes to Medina High School, which is half an hour's drive from here. She's a senior and valedictorian of her class. She wants to be an aerospace engineer and I am very proud of her. She was born in China in 1991 and she is eighteen years old.

We've been here on the ranch since December 2006. I love everything about the ranch—it is so beautiful here. I'm not sure if there is a typical day on the ranch. During the past two years I've cut cedar and pulled cedar. I really enjoy

Ambassadors of the

working outside. Then I run cows and I also like feeding cows. We had dogs who had some puppies and then we got chickens. I love my garden where I planted tomatoes and cucumbers for the first time in my life. I have a lot of time to read and to decorate the house.

But then I started feeling I needed to have a job, so I started teaching school in 2009 in Medina. I teach content mastery. This is a class for kids who need a little one-on-one in small groups. Maybe they don't understand well, or maybe they missed a test and this is where I come in and help them.

My daughter drives her own car to school because after that she goes to Schreiner University to take calculus and other college courses. She has been accepted to UT Austin but prefers to go to Harvard.

My husband still had to go overseas for a while to finish his projects, but he's finished now. We would be left here for a month or two, just me and my daughter. We have gates and our dogs would alert us if anything happened. Usually it's animals. I learned to shoot a gun, not that I ever used it. But you never know.

My husband was a project manager and he goes to remote locations, hardship locations, and he starts up projects. Then big companies come in when the ground is broken and they have somewhere to live with available water and supplies they need. They cannot come in and just start drilling. It doesn't happen like that—you have to build a camp and be prepared.

Americans who don't know me, ask all the time, "How did you, a Russian from Moscow, with all this background, all this diplomatic school, end up in Medina, Texas?" I usually tell them it was my husband's idea but I accepted it. I still think it was a good choice. The Russians don't ask because they met my husbands and they know the whole story.

My legacy to my daughters and the young people of today is a simple one. My oldest daughter is a Russian girl and Mary, my youngest, is a 100 percent American girl and she knows Russian, too. I tell my students they should always dream big. They have to go for it and they should never give up. There is nothing in the world they cannot do if they apply themselves. Nothing. It might take longer and harder work, but based on my experience, if I went by the book I shouldn't have left my country. If you dream big, if you believe in yourself, if you go for it and apply yourself, it will happen. It will.

MOUNTAIN HOME

Susanne Frenzel

Mountain Home, Texas–Gadderbaum, Germany

I grew up in a very small town in Germany. Back then we didn't have many cars to drive because it was just right after the war. I was born in 1958 so the conditions were pretty hard at that time. We were five children and I was the oldest, thus I had a lot of responsibilities early on. Only my father worked and my mother was at home. I guess she had enough work with five children. We didn't get a lot of meat on the table during the week because we had no meat. Our biggest meal was on Sunday. We lived right next to a big farm where we got fresh milk and eggs. We dug potatoes in the field, so it was a little tough growing up.

The school was about three miles away. Believe it or not, we walked both ways—winter, or summer, rain or shine. Sometimes we had no shoes. It sounds pretty unreal, but yeah, sometimes with no shoes. We had shoes when winter arrived. I had one summer dress and one pair of pants for the winter. We washed those clothes at night to have them ready the next day. We did not have a washing machine or dryer. Nobody had heard about a dryer back then. It was all right. At that time it was fun, I guess. When you are a child you don't care.

Some people in town had shoes because they lived better than us. It all depended on where you grew up, how many in your family, how much work you had, and how much income there was, just like everywhere else.

I really liked school and it was easy for me. I didn't have many friends growing up. I just went to school, went home, and helped my mother. I had a lot of chores and I didn't have time to play much. My chores were to wash clothes, clean the house, and make our beds. My mother was very strict and very organized. Back then I don't think we saw it as hard because it was normal for us.

As a teenager, we had to work even more. My mother took us once a week into the woods and we picked blueberries and blackberries. We all had big buckets and hauled mushrooms—it was a good time too. My brothers and sisters went also. I had to watch them because I was the oldest. I was in charge of them, too. With all the responsibilities, I didn't have any free time to enjoy what the other girls did, like shopping or going to the theater or anything like that. We were very limited in that department.

I was born in '58, so I was a teenager in the '70s. I was not very big on sports. At home I played soccer with my brothers and we climbed trees. Sports weren't big back then in school. It wasn't like it is today. We had gym class but it was mostly boring. My favorite thing always was reading. My father had a giant room full of books and I read every free minute I had. Another thing I did when I could was horseback riding on the neighbor's farm. That was real fun. Although I enjoyed riding horses, I don't ride anymore. I just gave my horse away.

After I finished school I went to a nursing school. I worked for a big hospital nearby in a large town. I went for their three-year nursing program and homemaking program. I became a homemaker. In Germany it was something you had to learn—you went to nursing, you went to classes for the home, you learned how to correctly iron your sheets, believe it or not. You also learned how to cook diabetic meals, etc. I specialized in housekeeping but had to have a degree for that in Germany, believe or not. It is a basic housekeeping degree certificate that says you went to school and you can be employed by a hotel or by a big household where they need someone to oversee the staff.

I only attended schooling there, and then I started working for a veterinarian. He needed me in his household and also in his practice, which I really enjoyed it. I helped him with surgeries like when a cow had her baby and at night when an animal was in trouble. I also helped him with his house and children. It was good work.

Following that job I sold jewelry for several years and traveled from town to town all over Germany. I went through every little town in Germany. A couple of years after that I decided to come to America. I had gone all over Europe including Spain and Italy and I thought I wanted to go to Texas. My father had a lot of books about Texas and we watched all those Western movies. It was

Ambassadors of the

just something that enticed me. Texas was it, the wide-open spaces, that's what I dreamed about.

I flew to Houston because I had a friend living there. She was married to a ship's captain. I knew her a little bit but not very well until I got there and we became friends. Shortly after, I met my future husband, an American living in Houston. He served in the Air Force in Germany previously. We were married for thirteen years. We were in Houston for several years where I had both my children. My daughters were born in Houston and Conroe. We then moved to San Antonio because he got a job as a mechanic and a salesman. I stayed home with the children.

From San Antonio, we moved to Rock Springs. We were fortunate because a garage came available to buy that included a tow service. We stayed there for six years. My children attended the Divide School for several years. They had only one school there with only one classroom with ten children in that school. I drove my children every day forty miles so they could attend this good school. I went to the school and visited with the teachers and I thought you could not find a better school. It was the best decision I've ever made. Usually, I dropped them off and I had to make a parts run into Kerrville for my husband's garage. I did my shopping in Kerrville, my parts run, and picked the children up after school. It all worked out.

After thirteen years of marriage, my husband and I decided to separate due to many different reasons. It just wasn't working for us. The children and I moved to Lazy Hills Guest Ranch and we were there almost four years. They hired me to be a cook. They always told me maybe God wanted me to go by there because they searched for a cook high and low and could not find one. They gave us a little house to live in and the girls and I stayed with them.

My youngest daughter attended Notre Dame Catholic School in Kerrville and my oldest attended Ingram schools. I met my second husband, who was living in San Saba and worked for the *Mountain Sun* newspaper in Kerrville. He wrote articles like "Up the Creek." I really met him when I was on a date with another gentleman. He just came over, interrupted us, and made a date with me. We were married for about a year. I think the idea of being married sounded good, but he traveled a great deal. The girls and I really loved him but it just did not work.

We lived in Hunt for a year while we were married and then after I moved back to Kerrville where I rented a little house next to Patrick's Lodge. I started a housecleaning business in Kerrville. I was on my own with two children. They both worked with me but they were still in school and very small.

While living in town I thought of several possibilities for us. I didn't want to live in town so I kept looking around until I finally found a place in Mountain Home, but there was no house on the property. The girls and I lived in a little shack out there for almost a year. It was just one room and it was used for hunting. There was no running water so we had to bathe in the water trough outside. Finally, I found this old house and I had it moved out here. I started working on it to make it livable.

After a year, my oldest daughter went to live with her father in Houston for maybe a year. My youngest and I just lived there and made the best of it. I could either put my money into this place to build another house or fix this shack up, or rent something in town, which would be money wasted. We decided to live in there. I have always wanted to live like this.

I wanted to have a bigger place but it just didn't happened. I love nature and animals. I have chickens, cows, and I get my own eggs. I also have a big garden. I have six cattle now and three babies. It's work, but I enjoy this kind of work.

My parents probably think I am crazy. When my children were little and I was married to my first husband, my parents came over to visit almost every year. After five or six years my mother's health didn't allow her to fly anymore so they stopped coming, but they really enjoyed it here. If they could have they would probably have moved here. But, my mother is real tight with her other children and grandchildren and it just didn't work out. All my family members still live in Germany and we keep in contact by sending each other photographs.

I always loved it here and I think I would have been a good pioneer woman because I feel wonderful when I am out on the plains. To this day I don't waste electricity or water and we are very careful with all the utilities. This winter we didn't even use our propane just wood and we have plenty of that on the property. I have been here about nine years.

My parents' background was quite interesting. My father had a different kind of job than most people. He made books, but didn't write them. He did bindings and put books together by hand. He was much sought after because it was a rare ability and not many people did that kind of work. That was his career and when no one wanted his handmade books anymore he had to re-learn; he went into computers. He was fifty-something and he did very well. He is retired now.

My mother always stayed home with the kids. Although my father was very strict he never spanked us because he only had to look at us and we knew. My mother was different. She sometimes threw her shoe at us if she couldn't reach us. They were honest and hard-working people and we had respect for them.

I met Floyd after I moved here about five years ago. A friend and I went to a motorcycle rally in Bandera and attended a party. He lived in Kerrville and was attending the same party so we got to know each other. We have been married for four years and he lives here on the ranch. He is a carpenter and is building that big beautiful building out there. Also, he works on a ranch between Comfort and Center Point. While he is working I make bread just like the pioneer women did during those early days.

I really enjoy everything about Texas—the open spaces, the weather is nice and warm, and the people. Also, I consider myself an environmentalist because back in Germany we were already recycling items we didn't need and taking bags back to the grocery store before I came here.

I used to rescue a lot of animals and I still have a kennel where I keep animals that people don't want until I find them new homes. I also help people who are in trouble or who need some money. I have helped a lot of them. I used

Ambassadors of the

to have a few girls working for me and they could always come to me if they needed something.

We help wildlife also. We have lots of deer, turkey, birds, squirrels, and fox. We had an exciting experience a while back when we let our chickens out and found a huge owl had eaten some of them. One night we heard a big racket and Floyd went outside with a flashlight and his gun and saw a large owl with a chicken in its talons. Although Floyd knew owls were protected he shot in the air and the owl let go of the chicken and it survived. I still have that chicken and all the chickens are now caged.

My career continues with my business of housecleaning. I go to Boerne, Fredericksburg, Harper, Mountain Home, and Ingram. It takes a long time to establish a clientele if you want to do it professionally. I only go by myself now—I used to have a girl work with me and I used to work for a couple of places where I had to hire a few girls and oversee them. But that was many years ago. I try to go the easier route now.

My oldest daughter cleans at the Museum of Western Art in Kerrville. She does the whole nine yards—sweeps and polishes the floor, dusts, and does everything there every day. I think she is doing a pretty good job and I hope I taught her right. My youngest daughter is a little artist. She likes to paint and do odd-and-ends jobs. Most of her paintings I have hanging in my home. She works usually as a waitress and sometimes she works for me. She also goes back and forth to Austin and California. She spends a lot of time in California as a waitress.

My legacy to my daughters, grandson, and the young people of today in Texas, the United States, and Germany is simple. The most important thing I think is respect. If you don't show respect to your neighbors, your children, to grownups, your parents, to the people that live on the land, you're already in the wrong and it doesn't work for you. Plus, you have to be honest with people, too. If you start things out with a lie it doesn't work. Hard work is the next thing. I would never have been able to afford this place, by myself, because nobody helped me with this, if I hadn't worked hard. And I worked hard all my life. I still work hard almost every day even though I am fifty-one years old. I hope that is what my children will do, but also enjoy their lives. Like my youngest does, she travels a lot and she is able to because she has no children yet. I just want them to grow up and be honest, hard-working people.

My final comment would be to enjoy yourself, too. Go out and dance and have a glass of wine or two. Enjoy your life because it's too short.

WARING

Ambassadors of the

Sharon McLaughlin

Waring, Texas–Hammond, Indiana

I am from Hammond, Indiana, which is at the tip of Lake Michigan, and I have lived in Texas for fourteen years. My husband is from Wisconsin. I was pushed and pulled to come to Texas because my husband was in the Air Force and he had one year left to finish his thirty years.

We lived in Alaska for some time. I spent a great deal of time at Denali Park because the Air Force base was in Fairbanks. If you looked southwest, there was the Alaskan Mountain Range. I could jump in the truck, which I did many times, with my cooler, my backpack, my cameras, and sleeping bag, and I'd spend two or three days there by myself while he was working during the summer. I have pictures that make my heart beat fast.

My husband spent seven winters in Alaska and was suffering from Seasonal Affective Disorder, which made him depressed. They finally sent us out. I didn't know where we were going. I would have loved to have gone to Montana or Wyoming or Colorado. But because we had a daughter and grandchildren in Boerne I said okay to Texas, for a year. I really thought I would be able to stay one year and then go back north to the mountains and snow.

It took a while, it truly took a while, but my attitude changed. In Alaska, I became an advocate for parks and wildlife as well as mountains. I had nothing to photograph down here except my grandchildren. My granddaughter was a cheerleader in high school and my grandson was a basketball player in middle school, so they were always in the paper. Although we had agreed to stay for a year, my husband, unbeknownst to me, had been watching the real estate section in the Boerne newspaper.

Then he found this place. However, he'd known about it for a year. He agreed that if I moved here he could make this my dream home. It was not the one that I had planned in Alaska, but one I could live in. I have pictures all over the house of mountains with lots of snow on them. I'm getting acclimated to the heat. I do a lot of things early in the morning in the garden, the yard, the bird and deer feeders.

Four months after I got here my daughter met a cowboy, fell in love, sold her ranch, and moved. So here I was with no daughter, no grandchildren, and it grew under my tail. Now, I love it. I realize I'm where God wanted me to be. I didn't love it at first, but I love the peace down here. We're not far from town. And my husband's health has improved tremendously—that's the main thing.

I have a sister who is two and a half years younger than me and my mom and dad. I grew up during World War II so it was a little tough at that time, but I had no idea about the conditions. We lived across the street from Grandma. My father worked long hours in an oil refinery. He worked the four to midnight shift a lot, so with me being in school during the day, I never saw him. Mom was a scout leader and she had us out enjoying nature all the time—that's why Alaska is so special to me.

Every Saturday morning when I was in eighth or ninth grade we'd write on slips of paper the five rooms in the house and put them in a bowl and draw to see which rooms we would clean. Because I was the oldest I got three rooms, and it never failed, I got the kitchen and the bathroom, which meant scrubbing floors. We couldn't go anyplace until those chores were done.

I don't remember much about school. My sister can tell me the day she went to kindergarten, what the linoleum looked like, and what the teacher talked about. I can tell you all my teachers' names but I can't recall much about my grade school years. In sixth grade I had a teacher who taught social studies and she made me want to be an archeologist. We studied about Greece and Egypt

Ambassadors of the

and I fell in love with that area. I tried to pursue that, but I never got too far. I was encouraged to go to a college preparatory high school but I had no desire to go to college at that time. I wanted to be a mother and a wife and I wanted to be just like my mother.

My boyfriend was going into the Air Force so we got married while I was still in high school. He left and I graduated from high school, and by this time I was expecting our first child. We moved to Syracuse where he went to Syracuse University Language School. He became a Russian linguist. I had my daughter in Rome, New York.

From Syracuse he went to Germany for a year and a half. Now, I want to tell you something funny. My daughter was born in October and at Christmas we went home on a train to Indiana. I was mesmerized by the snow. When we got to the train depot I told my parents I was going to find an attorney and sue them because they never told me snow was white. Because of the steel mill and the oil refinery I never knew this—it would melt and it was black. I didn't sue them, but I did live with them for a year and a half.

I was supposed to go to Germany with my husband and I had the money saved, then the Berlin wall was built. My husband had to carry a carbine just to walk to work so the family couldn't go. When he came back we went to San Antonio to Kelly Air Force Base. It was my first experience in Texas and I loved it. We got here at Thanksgiving and it was wonderful, but come Christmas I was speechless. Where was the snow? Where was the cold weather? It didn't feel like Christmas. I cried and cried. Well, Christmas got over and I lived through spring and summer. We had another Christmas and I cried again.

My husband got out of the service after four years because he didn't want to see me so miserable. I was more miserable because I missed the service. I missed the lifestyle and the traveling around. And who wanted to live with your parents again when you were married and had a child? So he reenlisted and they sent us right back to San Antonio for another year and a half. Come Christmas, I shut all the blinds and I turned on the air conditioner and I had some Christmas lights.

I loved being an Air Force wife and traveling around to other places. Seeing other cultures and other places was wonderful. The first chance I got to go any-place was to Alaska and by this time we had three children. Robbie was born in Omaha while we were at Offutt Air Force base and Jeffrey was born in Syracuse. When Jeff was eight months old we got an assignment to Japan, but my husband was stationed in what they call a POW camp at an Air Force base so I stayed in San Angelo with the children.

The military sent us to Alaska. To me Alaska meant snow all the time and I was loving it, because it was 113 degrees in San Angelo at that time. Lake Nasworthy was evaporating an acre or two a day. We went to the Fairbanks Air Force base and stayed in base housing and I loved every single bit of it.

I never worked while I was married, my husband wouldn't hear of it. He was a good old German man and told me, "I will take care of you." I believed him and I loved him. I was married for twenty-two years to that man, a dear man and the father of my children. But he couldn't imagine being a grandfather when our daughter married and he left me with two teenage boys.

I went back to school and became a medical assistant. My husband left three weeks after I graduated. I worked for two months for a doctor for $420 dollars a month. You can't raise two teenage boys and have a house and mortgage on $420 and whatever I got for child support. So I went to the employment agency and they told me there was a position open for a secretary. I'd been out of school for twenty-one years. I interviewed with a gentleman who gave me the break I needed. My typing wasn't fast enough and I'd been out of circulation, but he said, "Let's give it a try." I worked for Westinghouse Electric for four years and loved it. That was in Omaha, Nebraska.

Two years later I met Michael at a dance. I knew he had to be military because of his haircut. Turned out he was with my ex-husband's squadron. I walked out of the place and said, "No way Jose." But my first husband was a linguist and Michael was an electrician. They worked in two separate areas. Mike took care of the equipment that Bob worked on. Now I was back in the Air Force life and it was wonderful to be a part of the camaraderie.

I wasn't married yet but we he said I'd have to give him an answer because he could go to Germany, Okinawa, Greece, or Alaska. I told him go to Greece. He said, "All you talk about is Alaska." I knew some people turned to alcohol because of the long nights in Alaska and I had lived in Greece for two years. After several weeks he got his assignment—to Alaska!

I wasn't ready for marriage and I had a teenage boy yet to raise. My mother loved Mike and thought he was great, because he reminded her of my father. So I got married, but I wasn't happy about it. We had to travel fifty miles to Nebraska City to meet the judge at a park on Saturday. That morning I told my mother I didn't want to get married because I didn't love him the way you should love a man. I told Mike, but he convinced me to ride to Nebraska City with him and he talked for fifty miles. He said, "If you marry me I can make you love me as much as you love Alaska." He knew I was marrying him to go to Alaska. We've been married twenty-nine years and I love him more than I love Alaska, but it took a while.

I've fallen in love with Texas. The people in Texas are so friendly and that is wonderful. In Alaska, if it was 20 degrees below zero you had to stop on the road and help somebody. Here in Texas it can be anything and people stop on the road and help you. You become a Texan. If it ever snows heavily in Texas again you can blame it on me. I loved living here in 1985 when San Antonio got fifteen inches of snow!

My daughter is now fifty-three, and I have a forty-six-year-old son and a forty-four-year old son. My daughter, Laurie, and her family live in Wimberley. Robert and his family live in Dallas. Jeffrey and his family live the closest to me and his children keep me young. I believe children are the jewels God provides us while we're on earth. I also have a stepdaughter who lives in Fairbanks, Alaska. Counting my step-grandchildren I have eleven grandchildren and three great-grandchildren.

　　　　　　　　　Ambassadors of the

The legacy I would like to leave my children and grandchildren first is my belief in Jesus Christ, my Lord and Savior. I want them to know Him like I do and to feel secure and safe by the minute, by the hour because He's holding us by the hand. Secondly, I'd like them to be true to themselves. If they've got something they want to do, nothing is impossible if they work at it. And third, make the best of every day, find something good in every day.

WIMBERLY

Josie Bisett, Petroleum Engineer

Wimberly, Texas–County West Yorkshire, England

Be completely open-minded about the possibilities out there and think beyond the box.

Norma Gonzales-Hillan, Secretary

Uhland, Texas-Saltillo, Mexico

I want young people to have a dream and to work hard to make that dream come true.

Ambassadors of the

Lee Epstein

Wimberley, Texas–Brooklyn, New York

Everyone calls me Eppy. I was born in Brooklyn, New York, in the depths of Depression in 1934, and lived there for the first thirty years of my life. As a little kid living in Brooklyn everything revolved around the streets—we played in the streets with our friends while our parents sat on the stoops and on chairs in front of the houses to watch. Every two years or so my mother packed us up and took us to the country. We left the concrete city and went upstate into the Catskill Mountains area and spent ten weeks there.

Then in 1941 the war started. I was almost eight, just going into public school at that time. We had air raid drills and rationing. My uncle who lived with us went off to war in the Army. My grandfather lived with us, too, we were an extended family.

In 1944 I was afflicted with a very bad case of poliomyelitis, actually it was Polio Bulbar Poliomyelitis, and it was 98 percent fatal. I went into the hospital and awoke three days later. I was completely paralyzed and stayed in that hospital for three weeks, and then my mother arranged to have me taken to upstate New York to a small town called West Haverstraw to a hospital that was called the New York State Reconstruction Home. Today it's called the Helen Hayes Hospital. I went through heavy rehab for ten months, learning how to move my hands, my legs, and how to sit up, how to lie down—how to do everything.

I was ten years old when I went into the hospital and I didn't get out of bed until February 1945. On June 27, my mother came to the hospital and said, "It's time you came home." She told the nurses, "I'm taking my son home today. I want that paperwork done because I want to be on the bus leaving here in two hours."

Two hours later we took the bus to Manhattan to the Hotel Dixie, which was the precursor to the Port Authority Bus Terminal. We got on the subway and went into Brooklyn and we were waiting for the trolley. My mom said, "To hell with this, we're going to splurge," and we took a cab to our house.

All the kids were out of school when we got home, but my mother told them to leave me alone. She took me in the house—my aunt and cousins and grandmother were living in the same house—and my mother sat down in a chair and cried like a baby. You could just see the tension float out of her and she hugged me and said, "Next week you're having an ice cream party."

In 1947 I was thirteen, and that was the year of my Bar Mitzvah. We had it in the middle of a snowstorm. I no longer could participate in sports, which I had always wanted to do, because I was still handicapped. I decided at a very young age that there had to be a better way of dealing with this than to cry and mourn it so I developed a good sense of humor. I became a storyteller and a jokester. My dad had gotten me a harmonica when I was twelve and I decided I was going to become the best harmonica player you could imagine.

Between age thirteen and seventeen, I was in Thomas Jefferson High School in Brooklyn, and I graduated in 1951. School was hell. I was not able to do what other kids did and it held me back a bit. I used to act out. I grew up very fast because that year I was in the hospital. I was by myself and only saw my mother twice a week and my father once a week. I had to learn to cope with the world. I had to learn to make decisions for myself.

When I was seventeen I made a decision to go to college. At sixteen, I went to work in New York City in my uncle's shop as a floor boy. I had to join the

Ambassadors of the

union and at sixteen, in 1950, I was making $35 a week, which was a grown-up salary. I saved all my money so I could go to college.

I wanted to have a career in advertising. I met a professor named Howard K. Rice and he became a life-long friend. He talked me into coming to Long Island University in downtown Brooklyn and I started there in September 1951. I went through in four straight years and graduated in June 1955.

Coping comes naturally to a kid who is by himself and doesn't have his parents around. I didn't antagonize people, I learned to read them, and I was careful about the people I associated with. I coped by being understanding of other people. Listening to them and having fun with them, never making fun *of* them. This attribute brought me later in life to the career of clowning, which I've done for the last twenty years.

In 1990 my wife signed up for class in Clearwater, Florida to learn clowning, but she couldn't continue it so she asked me to take over and I did. It was just such a natural thing because I'd developed a clown persona. I learned everything there was to learn about clowning, including my own makeup. I started to perform as a clown in 1994, and I was invited to participate in the Orange Bowl festival. I was in the parade and also performed at half-time at the Orange Bowl football game with 150 other clowns.

I spent from 1961 to 2000 in the computer industry. I was an IBM executive during that time and for twenty years I had my own business. I've done consulting and I just enjoy learning new things.

I came to Texas because God and his wisdom said this is where I should be. In 1990, we sold our home on Long Island in a small town called Freeport and had an opportunity to be in business in Florida. We went there for five years. After that petered out, we visited my sister-in-law who had just moved to Wimberley. We drove down from Dallas to visit her. She understood we were looking to get out of Florida and said there was a house for sale right down the road. We met the owner and looked around, but it was a very, very small house on six acres. The price was ridiculously low, and my wife looked at me and she sort of nodded her head. That was on August 26, 1995 and we moved here January 9, 1996.

We had a wish list and one of the wishes was to live in the country and have a lot of acreage. Well, here was our opportunity and it just fell into our lap. We knew nothing about the area other than it looked nice. We hadn't met any people, but my sister-in-law kept telling us it was a great place to live with a lot of wonderful people—musicians, artists, sculptors, writers, and actors. She said, "You'll fit right in."

When I got to Texas I gained notoriety because everybody knows me as Eppy the clown in Wimberley. Kids still come up and say, "Hey, remember when you did my birthday party?" and I still do. Texans are open; they are warm; they are gregarious; they have a good sense of humor.

I make balloons at Lions Field on market day and I do the Wimberley rodeo. I do all kinds of affairs. I've become a member of the Board of Directors of the EmilyAnn Theatre here in Wimberley, which is a nonprofit organization. I've found when you live in a small town you get the opportunity to really shine and this is what's been happening to me in the last sixteen years. I've just blossomed, my music has flourished, my writing skills have flourished, my art has flourished, my magic and clowning have flourished. I want to continue with my music and do my clowning for as long as I can, as well as writing. Michelangelo, the great artist, when he was eighty years old said, "I am still learning," and that's my credo. I want to continue to learn.

To the young people of today, I would like to say: 1) live by the Golden Rule, do onto others as you would have others do onto you; 2) get yourself educated; 3) read and question what you read and don't take everything for granted; 4) don't be afraid to make decisions on your own.

Parents will come up to me with children four or five years old and ask me to make a balloon for their kids, and they want to tell the kids what to say and what to do. I tell the parents to let their children make their own decisions. I say, "You don't want to end up with a thirty-five-year-old kid living at home who can't make a decision because you wouldn't let him pick out a balloon when he was five." I work with children and make them feel they've accomplished something making decisions all by themselves. We forget there is a world that exists from our waists down that belongs to the children of this world. Treat them with respect and they will treat you with respect.

Ambassadors of the

John F. Aceti

Kerrville, Texas–Niagara Falls, New York

Author John F. Aceti was born in Niagara Falls, New York. He received his Bachelor of Science degree from the State University of New York at Fredonia, NY and his Master's from the University of Buffalo.

He retired to the Texas Hill Country in 1993 following a thirty-four year career as a teacher, school administrator, and educational consultant. He has written a number of articles for state and national administrative educational journals. He is also the author of several books.

He and his wife Carol have served as volunteers in China, Italy, and Poland as teachers of English as a second language. They have also participated in Mission Awareness Programs in El Salvador, Guatemala, Nicaragua, and Bolivia.

John serves as an active Rotarian at the club, district, and international levels. Both he and Carol participate in community organizations and church activities, and they enjoy traveling the world.